D1634808

EVERYDAY
ABOLITIONIST

Discover What You Can Do

To Help Stop Modern Slavery / Human Trafficking

TATE JOHNSTON

ISBN: 978-1-9999944-1-9

Everyday Abolitionist Press
LONDON

"I started reading, and it's so good I can't put it down!! Your writing is compelling and your content is quality. Thank you for putting this together . . . I love it. I love it. I love it!"

Christa Foster Crawford
Founder, Freedom Resource International

"If you are asking yourself, what can I *actually* do to combat modern slavery and human trafficking? Then hold on to your hat because *Everyday Abolitionist* will answer that question directly. Tate Johnston describes his journey in a deeply personal and practical way, and you'll be nodding involuntarily with each page you turn, and to each resource he points you to. If you are looking for an Abolitionist Bootcamp 101, *Everyday Abolitionist* has got to be in your training regime. And like all good training, it intensifies the further on you read. And FYI, no matter how long you have been an abolitionist, everyone would do well to read this book."

Peter Mihaere
Founder & CEO, Stand Against Slavery

"When you begin to understand the scope of modern day slavery, you find yourself with so many questions about what to do and how to respond. As you enter into the stories of real people who have suffered because of human trafficking, you end up with so much heartache and so many emotions. In *Everyday Abolitionist*, Tate Johnston is committed to helping you on this journey by providing concrete ways you can respond to both your internal emotions and the external needs. Sharing from his own journey while pointing you to excellent resources, this is a guide you will want by your side as you become an increasingly committed everyday abolitionist."

Kristen Deede Johnson
Award-winning Co-author
The Justice Calling: Where Passion Meets Perseverance

"*Everyday Abolitionist* is an essential book for activists learning about trafficking and other forms of modern slavery. It offers important insights just when it might feel awkward to ask as you learn about victims' experiences. But they need you to become a strong abolitionist if we're to see a world in which slavery no longer thrives. *Everyday Abolitionist* offers you much-needed support on that journey."

Joanna Ewart-James
Executive Director, Freedom United

"Tate Johnston's book *Everyday Abolitionist* is a must read for anyone who wants to learn and have a thoughtful and impactful response to the problem of modern day slavery. Besides pointing to excellent resources, Johnston creates space to reflect in order to empower real action in the fight against this global injustice. Invite a friend, take the time to pick this book up and read and discuss and act. You won't be disappointed."

"*Everyday Abolitionist* inspires you to change the reality of modern day slavery and human trafficking, to appreciate that each voice matters and to realize how every small action counts—whatever your age or your background."

"Insightful, inspiring, and loaded with practical resources—this book provides a well-thought-out plan to mobilize Everyday Abolitionists. For anyone who has ever wanted to *do something* about the evil of human trafficking, thank you, Tate, for proposing *how to begin.* We are grateful for and dependent upon *individuals* like you, who are willing to defend the dignity of everyone who 'sees the same sky'!"

TABLE OF CONTENTS

FOREWORD

Christa Foster Crawford

For nearly two decades now, human trafficking has been at the forefront of our minds when we think of the worst forms of injustice. The rise of the Internet and social media, combined with a newly-awakened call to justice among everyday people has brought about perhaps the greatest level of awareness in history to a problem that has existed since the beginning of time.

This awareness has sparked many to respond. Thousands of NGOs, social enterprises, ministries and governmental responses have been launched, and thousands more individuals have taken up the call to action overseas, and even in their own backyard.

But what is the average person to do if they are not currently in a position to or do not feel called to leave their home or change their job? For many, increased awareness has led to decreased clarity of how they should respond. At best, this awareness without clear pathways for response leads to compassion fatigue; at worst, it results in lost opportunities and wasted resources for substantive and sustainable change.

This book is about what every person can do—every day—to abolish trafficking. It explores specific areas in which the average person can make a difference. In which YOU can make a difference.

Whether you have long heard about human trafficking and have been wondering what to do, or whether this is your first introduction to the topic, *Everyday Abolitionist* offers important insights to responding, and responding well.

Christa Foster Crawford
Adjunct Assistant Professor of Children at Risk
Fuller School of Intercultural Studies
Founder, Freedom Resource International
February 2018

INTRODUCTION

What is *Everyday Abolitionist* about?

When I first learned about modern slavery/human trafficking, I was distraught, outraged, perplexed, paralyzed and overwhelmed with emotions. I felt isolated and unsure where to get answers or find out more, specifically, what I could do to make a difference.

Having gone on that initial journey of discovery (which I continue on), *Everyday Abolitionist* is designed to share what I've learned on specific topics. I want to help people be better informed and feel less isolated, to move from initial reactions to interconnected involvement, to move beyond awareness to taking informed action, addressing specific aspects of modern slavery/human trafficking.

There are a number of national or international one day or month long awareness raising initiatives. These are wonderful and important. One of the strengths of a single day is the focus it can bring. There may, however, be a gap in that, for those who are just finding out about trafficking, the single day or the whole month are either too brief or too long respectively. The focus is often that slavery still exists, the statistics and/or the question: what is human trafficking? The single day awareness initiatives, for which I am so grateful, are generating a lot of awareness, which is fantastic. But what then? How do people find out more? How can they move from general awareness to informed action? Do they understand the emotions and reactions they may be having?

The aim of this book is not primarily to raise awareness, though that may be a natural result of reading it, nor is it to explain human trafficking, to cover the statistics or to give an overview of the scope of modern slavery including specific instances and stories. Three books, *Disposable People* by Kevin Bales, *Sex Trafficking* by Siddharth Kara and *Not For Sale* by David Batstone, are all excellent resources if that is what you're looking for.

The aim of this book is to help everyday people move from human trafficking awareness to informed and empowered to take specific actions to stop modern slavery. *Everyday Abolitionist* covers specific topics related to modern slavery/human trafficking to help people understand various emotions they may experience, learn about potential pitfalls and discover specifically what they can do to help stop modern slavery/human trafficking.

How To Read *Everyday Abolitionist*

First, you may want to read *Everyday Abolitionist* with at least one friend or a small group of people so you have someone to process your thoughts and feelings with and to support one another as you read and reflect and ultimately take action.

Second, you may want to read the book one of two ways. Either:

A) Read a topic a day and reflect and talk with others, as well as taking any actions you'd like to take as a result. Reading a few topics a week may work well for sparking discussion at a weekly meet up with a friend or a group.

OR

B) Read it through at your own pace, whether that is in one sitting or over a period of time. Then, go back through the book and take time to consider one topic at a time over the course of a few weeks or more. Take time to reflect, chat with friends (maybe invite a few people to go on this learning journey with you) and explore the resources and take action.

Each day will feature one topic, such as Vicarious Trauma or Supply Chains, for example. I will share my thoughts, feelings or experiences. These are shared in the hope that people can relate to someone who has felt what they may be feeling or has asked the questions they may be asking. I will then share something I realized, was taught or learned, and point people to excellent organizations, further resources and next steps.

We won't stop trafficking in general unless everyday people consistently take informed actions to address specific aspects leading to and resulting from trafficking, unless everyday people move beyond awareness to learning and growing and doing what they can do, taking informed action to stop specific slavery in specific ways in specific places.

That is ultimately where *Everyday Abolitionist* ends and the rest of your journey begins.

If you'd like a little more background on my initial journey before we start, check out:

For Your Eyes Only: Here is My Heart . . . and Some Backstory (at freecember.org)

And, in case you're not sure this book is for you, but you do want to do something to stop modern slavery / human trafficking, here are a few things you could do and an invitation from me:

So... What Can I Do About Human Trafficking? 5 Simple and Specific Steps Anyone (Including Me) Can Take To Help Stop Modern Slavery (at freedomfortnight.org)

Or, perhaps, you're ready to begin.

If so, the Prologue awaits you.

I invite you to come on this possibly unexpected journey with me.

WHO AM I TO...?

"Pursue your heart for justice."

—Brian Christopher Berry

What right do I have to attempt to this? Wouldn't it be better if it were written by experts? Approved by organizations?

What right do I have *not* to try? To keep these thoughts and feelings to myself? To hoard what was so generously shared with me?

And, by the way, traffickers aren't waiting for anyone's permission to enslave people.

What credentials do I have? Only that once I found out about human trafficking and was overwhelmed with emotions, questions, urgency and determination.

And there were people willing to have conversations with me.

What *Everyday Abolitionist* Isn't

This isn't Human Trafficking 101. It's not about statistics or the differences between debt bondage and forced labor. It's not about different types of slavery such as child soldiers and domestic minor sex trafficking. It's not even about the gaps in provision, such as what happens once someone turns 18.

It's specific things I wish I knew when I was finding out about human trafficking.

What *Everyday Abolitionist* Is For

This book is designed to help people learning about human trafficking navigate the feelings and early questions that arise. It is designed to help you connect with others who care and point you to quality resources so that you not only know the statistics and realities, but also understand the emotions you may be feeling and can begin to get answers to your questions. And to let you know, you're not alone.

Who Am I To Write A Book About Modern Slavery / Human Trafficking?

Full confession: Um, not sure. I'm probably not qualified. There are a lot of things I'm not. I'm not an expert. I haven't worked in the field. I haven't been a slave. I'm not a survivor. I don't have any firsthand experience of slavery (that I know of . . . or have I?). I haven't rescued someone enslaved.

I grew up believing I was unique and special (Thanks, mom!). The truth is I'm an ordinary, everyday person. And at the same time, I am unique and special. Irreplaceable. No one else is me. I may be replaceable for what I can do, but as anyone who has lost someone they love knows all too well, I can't be replaced for who I am relationally, to my mom, my friends, my wife, my kids, for example.

No one else has your unique combination of skills, experiences, perspective, position and possibilities. Not even identical twins share all of those. Even if you had a clone, your clone wouldn't share your exact experiences and perspectives. Or relationships.

Think about it. Your clone wouldn't have itself as a clone, right?

Anyway, as Oscar Wilde said, "Be yourself. Everyone else is already taken." You might have heard it said if everyone is special, no one is special. I disagree. You are someone. You are some one. And by being one, you are special. Not for what you can do, but for being you. Unique. And so is everyone else on the planet. Everyone. Every. One.

So, I have no credentials that qualify me to write a book about modern slavery/human trafficking. Maybe other than this, I know what it feels like to find out unique and special human beings, children, women and men, are being coerced, manipulated, deceived, abused, used and discarded like . . . trash.

Like Kevin Bales' seminal book's title: *Disposable People*.

Like objects.

Worse than animals.

I know what it feels like to be wrecked by the reality of human trafficking.

Heartbroken.

Outraged.

Confused.

Overwhelmed.

Asking, "but, what can I *do!?*" What can I do that will actually make a difference? Will I always feel like this? Why isn't everyone talking about this? Does anyone else care about this like I care about this? Who are they? How do I find them? What should I do now?

And there are some things I had to go hunting to find out that I wish I had a way to find out faster. Maybe this journey is supposed to take time. Turning the tide on trafficking won't happen overnight.

Who am I? As the man in black said, "No one of consequence."

Or maybe, like he, I am. Someone of consequence. And you are, too.

What am I? A fellow human being. Heartbroken. Outraged. A little less confused. A little more hopeful. A little less overwhelmed. A little more connected. A little more informed. A little more determined.

To go beyond awareness. To take informed action.

And to invite, inspire, equip and empower others to take informed action, too. Widespread. Informed. Sustained. Effort. To stop slavery and help people at risk of/affected by trafficking.

So I will start where I am and do what I can to help people free people. No one can do everything, but everyone can do something. You are unique. You are special. You matter. You can make a difference.

Oh, and you're not alone. In how you feel. In your questions, doubts, hopes, fears, confusion and determination. And together, we can turn the tide on trafficking.

I'm learning. I'm taking steps. If you've picked up this book and you're still reading, you might just be taking your first steps in finding out about and fighting trafficking or you might be taking your next steps in fighting modern slavery and helping the people at risk of/affected by human trafficking.

Wherever you are on your journey, I'm glad you're here.

Let's continue this journey together.

Who am I?

No one of consequence?

What do I have?

What I have is a heart for helping people at risk of/affected by human trafficking, funding the frontlines organizations addressing it, and empowering everyday people to help stop modern slavery.

I'll try to keep this short and sweet:

Here's the deal. I'm a 40 something, white, Western male, "in between jobs" and just got my Master's Degree. Never been trafficked or enslaved. Not a survivor, celebrity or CEO. You might see the limitations of my perspective and/or position. I can't change that. I can only start where I am with what I have and who I am.

During this journey of discovery, I have been overwhelmed, outraged, perplexed, distraught, confused, paralyzed and determined. I've asked loads of questions, taken classes, read research, written poetry and posts, run hundreds of miles and helped people raise over $25,000 for International Justice Mission (IJM), Saving Innocence, A21, Not For Sale, Hope for Justice, WMFBolivia and HUG Project.

Not millions, but not nothing.

Once, I went searching for companies producing ethical clothing and placed a $350 order that helped prevent a family from being in a situation where they could have been facing the decision to sell their teenage daughter. Are you kidding!? $350!? To help an ethical company employ a parent so they don't have to face that dreadful decision!?

So there are my credentials: I've spent the past 4 years actively seeking to answer the question, "But what can I *do*?!"

I'm on this journey. I've been wrecked by emotion. I've asked questions. I've learned. I've taken action. I've asked more questions. I've had the privilege of talking with people further along in the journey who gave me insights I wish I knew earlier and I'm glad I now know. I've studied and gotten a Master's Degree with a focus on Children at Risk. And I've helped other people take some next steps, too.

So, if that's credentials enough for you, I invite you to come on this *Everyday Abolitionist* journey, a kind of "things I wish I knew when I first started caring about human trafficking." Hopefully, I'll be the lead learner, your guide at the side.

As we get ready for the first day/chapter/topic, I'd like to encourage you one more time to invite at least one other person to join you.

I'll wait right here for you to reach out to them. Promise.

. . .

Okay, I hope they decide to join you!

Either way, let's get started!

Let's take the next steps toward helping stop modern slavery/human trafficking.

Let's move beyond awareness together.

PART I

PREPARATION

One

BEYOND AWARENESS

"Nothing happens just because we
are aware of modern day slavery,
but nothing will ever happen until we are."

—Gary Haugen, International Justice Mission

As you are here, you probably think human trafficking needs more attention. I agree. Awareness has been growing over the past decade plus, but there is still more to do.

When I was wearing my "upside down," purple, modern slavery awareness ribbon for a recent Freecember (freecember.org), an initiative to help raise awareness and funds for anti-trafficking organizations, a young woman asked what it was for and I said, "It's for modern slavery awareness." She looked at me quizzically. "Did you know there are millions of people enslaved in the world today?" I asked. "I had no idea," she replied.

In 2004, Kevin Bales, one of the pioneers in bringing public awareness to the issue, wrote *Disposable People: New Slavery in the Global Economy*. In the introduction to the revised edition in 2012, he wrote, "Around the world we still face the terrible frozen face of ignorance. *The awareness that there are twenty-seven million slaves in the world has not yet fully penetrated the public mind, but the sparks and fires of committed people are beginning to melt that icy apathy"* (italics added).[1]

The good news is, some more years on, there are even more sparks and fires of committed people. Some great people and organizations, such as Freedom United, END IT Movement with their Red X, the A21 Campaign via their Walk for Freedom and the CNN Freedom Project, are bringing human trafficking to the attention of massive amounts of people.

Maybe you've joined in and posted or shared on social media or walked, because this is important to you and it's something you can do to raise awareness.

Awareness is vital, because it's the beginning.

Joanna Ewart-James, Executive Director of Freedom United, the world's largest anti-slavery organization, mobilizing millions globally to speak up and take action, highlights how crucial awareness is in bringing about change:

> "To live in a world in which slavery no longer thrives, we must be in a society which does not tolerate exploitation and modern slavery. Values must be

adjusted. This is social change. Social change will happen when enough people stand up and make clear that modern slavery is a problem that needs to be addressed. A blind eye is no longer the response to the neglected and poorly dressed child who doesn't go to school, investigations are triggered for next door's domestic worker who never seems to be allowed out, and a 'good deal' raises questions about the conditions of workers involved in bringing that product or service to market. As individuals in society, our understanding allows us to challenge business as usual. This is why awareness is so important."[2]

Awareness is essential.

It's the prerequisite to gathering a movement of "enough people."

And I wholeheartedly agree with Gary Haugen, founder of International Justice Mission, who said, "Nothing happens just because we are aware of modern day slavery, but nothing will ever happen until we are."

Awareness is the first step, but if it's the only step, it's a wasted step: full of sound and fury, signifying nothing. We have to move beyond awareness.

So the challenge is answering your question and mine: how I can help from here? That's the purpose of *Everyday Abolitionist*, to help you move beyond initial reactions or emotions, beyond awareness, to help you avoid potential pitfalls and to discover what you can do to help stop modern slavery/human trafficking.

As a reminder or in case you skipped straight to "One," here's the deal. With the goal of laying a firm foundation from which to work, each day/topic, I'll share something I've learned on the journey and suggest a resource (or more) and an action (or more). These are optional. You can simply read along each day. Or you can take the time to explore the resource(s) or take at least one action after each topic. I guarantee if you do, this will be a much more significant and meaningful journey. To help a bit, I estimate the time each resource or action would likely take.

This journey can, at times, be a difficult one, so I have learned to focus on taking it bit by bit. As a Chinese proverb reminds us: "To get through the hardest journey we need take only one step at a time, but we must keep on stepping."[3]

My hope is that you can benefit from what I've learned on my journey so far and that your journey from where you are will be shortened and informed. And when the journey is hard, the things you learn from reading *Everyday Abolitionist* will be part of a foundation that will help you keep on stepping.

ACT: *ONE*

LEARN

Watch Kevin Bales' TED Talk (20 minutes)

Kevin Bales gave an amazing TED Talk in Feb 2010 called "How To Combat Modern Slavery."

I have a lot of respect for Kevin Bales and his pioneering work in the field of anti-slavery. After his TED Talk, I just don't think I know any more about what to do, though. I think it is simply mistitled and should be called: Modern Slavery 101: What Exactly Is Modern Slavery? So, don't expect an answer to what you can do, but take the opportunity to get a good sense of what modern slavery is and some of the dynamics at play.

INTERACT

Share What's on Your Heart & Mind With One Person (5 – 30 minutes)

Have a conversation with someone (or two). Share what's on your heart and mind with them. Share what you're learning and/or feeling. Listen to their heart or experience. Be willing to accept that other people aren't in the same place as you. They may not be at a place to join you on the journey. That's okay. Have some more conversations.

ACT

Join in:

- END IT Movement (enditmovement.com)
- A21 Campaign's Walk for Freedom (a21.org/walk)
- CNN Freedom Project's #MyFreedomDay (cnn.com/myfreedomday)
- Freedom United (freedomunited.org)
- Youth Underground (youth-underground.com)
- YouCanFreeUs (youcanfree.us)

everydayabolitionist.co

If you'd like another way to share what you're thinking or feeling in response to this chapter or to find out what others are thinking or feeling, you can visit or comment at everydayabolitionist.co/book/ch1

Also, because resources are being created and improved, I've set up a page for each chapter, where you can look for new and current resources. Or, if you're aware of a good resource, you can suggest one in the comments on the page for the relevant chapter, such as everydayabolitionist.co/book/ch1 or for consideration at everydayabolitionist.co/resources

Two

EVERYDAY PEOPLE NEEDED

(ON DOUBT AND FEELING INSIGNIFICANT)

"It took some time for me to understand that what the movement really needed was more everyday people. Regular moms, dads, grandparents, teachers, nurses, dentists, accountants, professors, business owners, senior citizens, physical therapists, doctors, janitors, bartenders, artists—anyone without a fancy title or who thought they didn't have any power . . . What was missing in the new abolitionist movement was people like me.

"What was missing was people like you."

—Kimberley McOwen Yim, *Refuse to Do Nothing*

When I first began really looking into human trafficking and made the decision to find out what I could do about it, it wasn't long before I had doubts. I wanted to make a difference, and I wanted that difference to be significant. When it comes to millions of people enslaved, I want every single one to be free!

And then I looked at myself: who am I to do something, anything to address slavery? (We can't all work fulltime for an anti-trafficking organization. I know. I've applied.) Maybe you're not doubting your ability or capacity to make a difference right now, but in case you are, or in case you do in the future.

One day, I wrote these words:

> *Who am I?*
>
> *What difference can I make?*
>
> *"You're just a minnow in a huge ocean."*
>
> *Honest and true words, spoken in the tone of a realist.*
>
> *Alone, I am small.*
>
> *But am I insignificant?*
>
> *What can one person do?*
>
> *Am I on a wild goose chase?*
>
> *But . . .*
>
> *Have you ever felt simply and utterly compelled to do something?*
>
> *In the face of proverbial overwhelming odds?*
>
> *But . . .*
>
> *What if?*
>
> *What if one becomes three?*

What if three become 30?

And 30 become 300?

What can 300 do?

(My friend, both history teacher and film fan can tell you. Heard of Thermopylae?)

I am only one.

But . . .

I can't not.

I simply cannot not.

I must.

I am compelled.

The same woman that said, "No one is free until everybody is free," also said,

"Three people that care are better than no people that care."

And I am not alone.

In some ways, I feel like I am late to the fight.

Many fires are already burning.

Not only people in non-profits like IJM, Not for Sale, Polaris Project & Love146, but people in governments and corporations and small businesses. And in families and twos and threes. And Tom and Emily.* (not their real names)

Yes, Tom and Emily. Two young people you've never heard of. Inconsequential? (I do not think that word means what you think it means.) Who have been getting together with a group of seven people for two years. Who hosted a screening of a movie followed by a panel with the London Metropolitan Police, IJM,

Hope for Justice & Sophie Hayes Foundation.

Tom & Emily.

Who put up posters and passed out postcards.

Who kept striking flint to tinder.

And rekindled a spark.

In me.

Bring on the reinforcements!

"Three people that care are better than no people that care."

Find two allies, friends, brothers and sisters in arms.

Light a fire where you are with what you have.

Am I a minnow? Perhaps.

Do I feel like one? Often.

But, I am a spark.

Only a single spark.

Alone, I cannot light a pitch-dark room.

Alone, I give no warmth.

There are many things I cannot do alone, but I can ignite a match that lights a flame that becomes a torch. I can be blown across rivers, over walls, through chain links and behind bars . . . igniting tinder until beacon fires burn in hearts and bellies, villages and cities, until a wildfire sweeps across fields filled with thorns.

I am potential.

Within me is the fire . . . and the flood.

I know there is a flood within me because every time I think about or write about modern slavery, the floodgates open.

A tear. Then weeping. Sobbing. Sometimes uncontrollably. In public.

There is a spark of life in every woman, man and child in slavery. An ember.

Perhaps it is only smoldering.

Being smothered.

Almost extinguished.

There is a spark in you, too.

(As I write these words, tears roll slowly down my cheeks. I'm sobbing . . . in public again. I can't not.)

. . .

Who am I?

Unknown?

Definitely.

Inadequate?

I feel like it.

Insignificant?

No.

What difference can I make?

A spark.

A drop.

By themselves, seemingly impotent.

But,

Without the spark, there is no fire. Without the drop, there is no ocean.

Let us become the fire & the flood.

ACT: *TWO*

REFLECT

Express Yourself (3 – 30 minutes)

When you think about 24.9 – 46 million people enslaved today, what are your thoughts or feelings? Write, draw, paint or share your thoughts/feelings with someone who listens well.

CONNECT

Don't Do This Alone (15 – 45 minutes)

Have some more conversations. Connect with others on a justice journey. Maybe you already know someone. You've seen their post or heard them talk about it before. Email, text, message, reach out to them.

Some people may give you blank looks or change the conversation. That's okay. We're all in different stages or may not be interested in or ready for this particular journey.

Keep going til you find someone else that cares, too.

Together, find a third.

Once you have three people, begin talking about what you'll do about it.

I could give suggestions, but not yet.

I don't want to limit your thinking.

By joining in, it's addition.

Twogether can be multiplication.

Threegether has the potential to be exponential.

Three groups of three is nine.

Three sets of three groups of three is 27.

Three of those? 81

One more time? That's heading toward 300.

Don't underestimate the power of three. (Some say it's the magic number.)

INSPIRATION

Read these quotes (2 – 5 minutes)

"I am only one, but I am one. I cannot do everything, but I can do something."—Edward Everett Hale

"Nobody made a greater mistake than he who did nothing because he could do only a little."—Edmund Burke

"Three people are better than no people."—Fannie Lou Hamer

If you want to go fast, go alone. If you want to go far, go together.—African Proverb

Does one of these quotes stand out to you? Inspire or encourage you?

Write down or share what you're feeling, thinking or learning.

RESOURCE

Book – *Refuse to Do Nothing: Finding Your Power to Abolish Modern-Day Slavery* by Shayne Moore & Kimberly McOwen Yim

INTERACT

Watch a Movie (90 mins to an evening)

Consider scheduling a film screening such as *Kavi, Lion, Slumdog Millionaire* or another film you know of. It could be you and a couple friends or something more organized.

Follow it with a formal or informal discussion with a few friends or a large group or panel.

Watch a Trailer (3 – 15 mins)

Visit everydayabolitionist.co/films to look for new and current short or feature length films or trailers. Or, if you're aware one, you can suggest it in the comments at there or submit it for consideration at everydayabolitionist.co/resources

everydayaboltionist.co

If you'd like another way to share your reflections or thoughts on Chapter 2 or to find out what others are thinking or feeling, you can visit or comment at everydayabolitionist.co/
book/ch2

Three

A BRAVE REFUSAL

(VICARIOUS/SECONDARY TRAUMA)

"The world is full of evil and lies and pain and death, and you can't hide from it; you can only face it. The question is: when you do, how do you respond? Who do you become?"

—Agent Coulson, Marvel's Agents of S.H.I.E.L.D.

When you started finding out about human trafficking, what was your initial reaction? Did you want to look away? Ignore it or pretend it isn't happening? Were you dumbstruck, outraged or distraught?

If you've had some conversations over the past few days, weeks or months, you'll know that when human trafficking is mentioned, different people have different reactions and feel various things.

One of the things most people initially or eventually feel is overwhelmed. People can feel overwhelmed for a few different reasons.

One means "I'm overwhelmed and I actually don't want to or can't bring myself to think about this" (right now, at least). Maybe it's because it can be such a heavy, even brutal, topic. Or because it's so massive and "I feel like I can't do anything to make a difference, so I won't think about it."

Recently, someone asked me what I was working on. I described an initiative called Freedom Fortnight (freedomfortnight.org) and my hope to help people move beyond initial awareness of human trafficking or emotional reactions. "For example," I explained, "initial reactions such as 'I don't even want to think about this,'" and she said, "That's where I am." Honest. Understandable. And then she changed the subject.

Maybe it's not the right time for her. Or she hasn't had the right resources, approach or support. Or maybe human trafficking will be a topic she always avoids. Or maybe she has other reasons. Not for me to judge or necessarily even know or pretend to understand.

Human trafficking can be unpleasant, uncomfortable, unsettling. Choosing to address it takes what Gary Haugen describes as a "brave refusal to look away."[1]

For me, that refusal and the choice to look further into human trafficking resulted in the second kind of overwhelmed.

The second kind of "I'm overwhelmed" is an emotionally overwhelmed, a "heartbroken, wrecked and my emotions are out of my control" overwhelmed. An "I'm so outraged and/or distraught" overwhelmed. An "I can't stop weeping" overwhelmed.

When I really started looking into doing something about trafficking, I had a lot of questions, and I started reading everything anyone recommended and anything I could get my hands on. Suffice it to say, I read a lot. And I wept a lot.

Then, I had a conversation with a friend of a friend named Wendy Dailey. She is the co-founder of International Sanctuary & Purpose Jewelry, a business that employs survivors of sex trafficking. I told her a little about my experience. She said something I'll never forget, "Stop reading the stories." Huh? I was a little stunned at first. Wait. What? And then she said, essentially, once you know about the realities of sex trafficking, stop reading the stories and decide to take action.

I don't remember much else about that conversation, but it was like I had been given permission not to traumatize myself with any more stories, while at the same time continuing the brave refusal to look away.

What I didn't realize and learned later in a Master's Degree course on working with sexually exploited and trafficked children, is that I was basically subjecting myself (unnecessarily) to something called vicarious trauma.

Vicarious trauma, or secondary trauma, if you're not familiar with it, can happen to people who "hear distressing stories, and witness violence, poverty and disaster. This second-hand exposure to suffering places them at high risk of experiencing secondary stress responses."[2]

Did you catch that? Just hearing distressing stories can cause vicarious trauma. It's not something that happened to you. You weren't even there. But you feel echoes of what the person felt, empathically. And you experience trauma of your own.

So, I stopped reading the stories. I stopped unnecessarily traumatizing myself by reading the stories of people who had experienced the trauma involved in being trafficked.

Later on, I found that I wasn't crying anymore when I thought about human trafficking. As much as I was glad I wasn't uncontrollably or spontaneously weeping, I wondered, "what's up with that? Don't I care anymore?"

A few months later I wrote:

> *Is There A Weeping Phase?*
>
> *It's been a while since I cried about the women and girls enslaved in sex trafficking.*
>
> *Maybe about a month or so.*
>
> *I thought maybe my weeping stage had run its course. Maybe there was another stage after the initial days of sobbing and crying in public when the realities become more matter of fact.*
>
> *I was wrong.*

For the past few days I've been reading The Hole in our Gospel, *reading about God's heart for the poor, the need and some rays of hope.*

Deep into the section on the difficulties and obstacles poor people face, deep in the thickets of hunger and thirst, the devastation of diseases such as malaria, tb and hiv/aids, the struggle and strangling force of lack of resources, all of which I read with a sense of despair and sadness, it was when I read "Some two million children, mostly girls as young as five years old, are part of the growing commercial sex trade around the world" that I began weeping again.

No specific heart-wrenching story. Not a book specifically about sex trafficking. In the middle of straightforward explanation of the realities of poverty, disease, and hunger, what absolutely breaks my heart is the children and young women abused and enslaved in sex trafficking.

. . .

Then, about a month after that I wrote:

No Emotion. Now What?

Between Half The Sky *and* The Locust Effect, *many tears were shed.*

And now I'm certainly more aware when things come on the news. I just saw something on BBC about child brides and fistulas this week.

Definitely, definitely tough. I've been wrestling through lots of emotions. And also wrestling about when I'm not overwhelmed with emotion.

. . .

So, I've been completely overwhelmed with emotion and I have also wrestled with not being overwhelmed with emotion. I'm cautious about exposing myself unnecessarily to stories while at the same time retaining a brave refusal to look away. I'm also cautious regarding the use and abuse of stories in awareness raising. (We'll look at that topic next.)

Just knowing about vicarious trauma has helped me understand what was happening to me. I'm now aware of the possibility of further vicarious trauma and can recognize when I might be experiencing it. I can also take steps to appropriately minimize the likelihood of vicarious trauma or to recover from it.

I know I'm not alone. I know because I shared about my weeping with a good friend of mine, who said, "Yeah, that happened to me, too. About a year ago." So if this has happened to you, you're not alone. Hopefully, understanding a bit more about vicarious trauma can help you navigate it or get to help. Understanding can also help you be sensitive to others who may have different reactions when the topic of human trafficking comes up or if they experience vicarious trauma.

ACT: *THREE*

REFLECT

Emoji (3 – 10 mins)

Have you felt strong emotions as you've learned about or begun working to address trafficking? What emoji best represent(s) what you've felt/are feeling? Think or write about your experience.

LEARN

Watch (3 mins)

Watch the video "What Is Vicarious Trauma?" by Dr. Laurie Pearlman of the Heading Institute, which explains Vicarious/Secondary Trauma

Read (5 – 10 mins)

An explanation of vicarious trauma: *Vicarious Trauma* (Excerpted from Understanding and Addressing Vicarious Trauma) by Dr. Laurie Anne Pearlman and Lisa McKay, Headington Institute.

REFRESH

Schedule (3 – 5 mins)

Is there something that refreshes you? A walk? A shower?
Art? Coffee with a friend? Something else? Schedule time
for it.

RESOURCE

Workbook (20 – 60 mins)

Take time to reflect and answer the questions in the
workbook Understanding & Addressing Vicarious Trauma:
Reflection Questions Workbook by Dr. Laurie Anne
Pearlman & Lisa McKay

INSPIRATION

Watch (15 mins)

Shannon Keith's TEDx Talk "Why I Turned Toward Sex
Slavery"

everydayaboltionist.co

Share resources, reflections, thoughts or feelings on Chapter 3 or find out what others are thinking or feeling by visiting or commenting at everydayabolitionist.co/book/ch3

WHAT TO BE AWARE OF AS YOU RAISE AWARENESS

(THE REAL RISK OF RE-EXPLOITATION)

Have you ever put your foot in your mouth or posted something on social media that you later regretted? Have you heard the phrase, "the road to hell is paved with good intentions?" Have you ever thought: I wish I had known that before I . . .?

I live in London, England but as I began investigating human trafficking and exploring what I could do, I visited some friends in Wichita, Kansas. While I was there, I had the opportunity to meet with Karen Countryman-Roswurm, a professor who leads the Center for Combating Human Trafficking at Wichita State University. (Did you know that Wichita is a crossroads for human trafficking in the U.S.A.? I didn't.)

After meeting with her, sharing my heart and listening to her counsel, she gave me a few "reading assignments." (She is a professor after all.) One was entitled "At What Cost: The Road To Anti-Trafficking Is Paved With Good

Intentions," about good intentions gone horribly wrong in anti-trafficking efforts, about a time someone was devalued and demeaned, and . . . Well, you should read the post. Boy, am I glad she shared it with me, before I unintentionally did something like what's described. Of course, out of the best intentions.

Later, in a graduate level class on working with sexually exploited and trafficked children, my professor and expert in the field of anti-sex-trafficking, Christa Foster Crawford, shared,

"I was at an anti-trafficking event recently and a survivor talked about how she felt that some anti-trafficking organizations were 'pimping her story.' Many times this is exactly what is going on—we are in a very real sense re-exploiting them (using them for our organization's financial gain or for the movement's spread). I am horrified, therefore, to read in the GEMS article that 'staff at a large organization that works on trafficking and gender-based violence tell me laughingly that they were going to be my "new pimps".' Disgusting! Let us all avoid doing this, even unwittingly."[1]

I'm glad I was made aware of this early on, before I really began to try to help raise awareness or did this "even unwittingly."

Shockingly, I have also been told of some coercive "techniques" in fundraising for anti-trafficking such as closing the doors of an anti-trafficking film screening and having people stationed so that viewers couldn't leave!

In our efforts to stop exploitation, we must not resort to the methods of exploiters, which include deception, manipulation and coercion.

This applies as we consider both the people we *intend* to help and the people we *invite* to help. This is something we must be aware of as we raise awareness. Our awareness raising shouldn't resemble a hostage situation or a drive-by shooting.

Another pitfall in raising awareness is to unthinkingly utilize inappropriate images. These can be unnecessarily sensual, imply skewed power-dynamics, or give false impressions of what trafficking is. Love 146 shares some in a post entitled "Anti-Trafficking Fail."

We must also be careful about sharing images of victims or survivors. That's part of the trickiness of anti-trafficking: sharing images of people at risk of/affected by trafficking could re-exploit them or put them at risk of being re-trafficked.

So, let's be mindful of images we share, post, re-post, use on websites, in social media campaigns, at events or presentations, or any kind of art (visual or otherwise) that we might create to raise awareness or funds.

I think of the medical oath, which begins: First, do no harm. I used to think not harming was a strange priority for people committed to healing, but now it makes more sense. In our efforts to help, let us commit to be mindful not to hurt.

We must be careful not to cause unnecessary harm (trauma) to previous victims, potential supporters, even "innocent bystanders" who see or hear our messages.

So I am left to contemplate how to be informative and appropriately persuasive without being unnecessarily graphic, deceptive, manipulative or coercive.

For me, when it comes to raising awareness, I think the most appropriate word is invitation. An invitation is an offer. It's not even a request. "Would you like to learn more about human trafficking?" If someone declines an invitation, it might feel like rejection, but you don't send people to drag them along or coerce.

By all means, let's invite people to join us in stopping trafficking. Let's just make sure that we're inviting with integrity and respecting survivors, victims and potential allies in the process.

ACT: *FOUR*

LEARN (5 mins each)

1) Read this post by Rachel Lloyd, founder of GEMS: At What Cost: The Road To Anti-Trafficking Is Paved With Good Intentions

2) Read this article on imagery by Love146: Anti-Trafficking Fail

NEXT LEVEL (30 mins)

Read this peer-reviewed professional journal article in the Journal of Human Trafficking: Awareness Without Re-Exploitation: Empowering Approaches to Sharing the Message About Human Trafficking by Karen Countryman-Roswurm & Bailey Patton Brackin

REFLECT (3 – 10 mins)

Look at an anti-trafficking post, website, article or image. What does it "say" about trafficking and the people involved?

INTERACT (4 mins)

Watch the short video My Story, My Dignity (4 mins)

Then, if you want to (on the same page), call on media to respect survivors and their stories.

And/Or take the My Story, My Dignity Pledge (1 min)

everydayaboltionist.co

Share resources, reflections, thoughts or feelings on Chapter 4 or find out what others are thinking or feeling by visiting or commenting at everydayabolitionist.co/book/ch4

Five

LANGUAGE MATTERS

Victim, Slave, Survivor, Prostitute, Sex Worker, Prostituted Person, Man, Woman, Child, Leader, Person, Human Being

It probably goes without saying all these words have definitions (big word for that = denotations). You probably realize they are all connected with certain impressions (fancy word for that = connotations) or evoke certain mental images or feelings. Have you taken time to think about the difference these words have in influencing how people think, feel or act (implications)? Or that they can even have legal implications?

Thinking about the language we use is an important step in being intentional as we address human trafficking. At the end of this discussion, we may disagree or choose to use different language. That's okay. The important thing is that we can be intentional about it.

Different words may be appropriate or necessary in different stages or contexts. For example, although it may be more appropriate in anti-trafficking circles to talk about *recovering* victims (that is, helping people exit situations of trafficking, sometimes referred to as "rescuing" victims), people outside or new to the anti-trafficking space may think *recovering victims* are people that are going through a restorative phase, like someone getting better after surgery.

So while recovery may be more sophisticated and nuanced than rescue because it respects the will and self-determination of the person enslaved, it might not make sense to the general public. People who are drowning, shipwrecked, lost in the wilderness or in a building on fire are rescued. Most don't get offended when someone uses the word rescue to describe what happened. And, although, it doesn't imply anything about their agency (i.e. the will and ability to act), rescue just seems more straightforward.

In discussing the terms recovery and rescue, I used the word victim. Did you notice? How did it make you feel? Did you think, "They're not victims, they're survivors!" What about this? They're not only survivors, they're people.

Is there a point at which someone doesn't want to be labeled according to what was done to them or something they experienced in the past? Or maybe they do sometimes and don't sometimes. Could that be their prerogative? And what if using the word victim makes it clear (even after they have survived the situation) that they were not responsible for what was done to them or even for what they did when they were in the situation?

Hope For Justice explains:

"Q: Is it a good idea to use the term 'victim'?

"Due to the manipulation, deceit, coercion and grooming employed by traffickers many people removed from exploitation do not realize they have been a victim. Understanding that what has happened to them is wrong and that the trafficker is to blame can be an important part of their recovery. Getting the general public and organizations to understand that a crime has been committed and that the crime has a human cost also justifies the use of a commonly understood term such as 'victim'. This is why Hope for Justice use the term 'victim', although staff remain aware of the sensitivities of such a label and will use the terms 'survivor' or 'client' when interacting with victims."[4]

(By the way, see how *recovery* could be a tricky word? Hope For Justice used it in the sense of making progress in a process of restoration rather than removal from a situation of being trafficked.)

Language matters. Language is powerful. It can have massive implications for laws and law enforcement, legislation and court rulings, for how we feel and think (about ourselves and others) and for how we act. For example, a 12 or 16 year old referred to as a prostitute in legislation, training manuals or conversation is likely to be treated very, very differently by police, judges and just about anyone who interacts with her or him, than if the child is thought of as a child victim of trafficking.

We may disagree about what words to use, but we can understand that someone else might be using a different word for a different reason in a different context.

Ultimately, I think it's about thinking through implications and having an attitude of respect.

Respectfully yours . . .

. . .

After I wrote this, I wanted to ask the insights of someone better placed than me to have an opinion on the matter. A professor of mine connected me with Harmony (Dust) Grillo, who founded Treasures, a survivor-led organization. I shared what I wrote on this topic with her to get her feedback and see if I was off on my thoughts regarding language. I'm on a learning journey, too, right? I was grateful to learn from her perspective and thought you might be, too. Here's what she wrote to me, in full, which I share with her permission:

> Hi Tate,
>
> First of all, I am really glad that you are addressing the need for thoughtfulness with regard to the use of language here. It is an important topic.
>
> I personally have very strong feelings about the word "rescue" as it relates to this movement. I find it to be overused and misused especially by people doing fundraising. People like the idea of rescuing and they like to be rescuers. However, more often than not, unless people are actually joining swat teams on trafficking ring busts, what they are doing is not really rescuing. The use of this word can also be disempowering as it places us in a one-up position as it defines the working relationship as rescuer-victim.
>
> To complicate matters further, due to trauma bonds and a whole other host of psychological chains, most women and girls who are "rescued" from their traffickers and exploiters end up going right back to them.

In my personal opinion, we are better off positioning ourselves as partners on their journey to freedom than rescuers.

In case it is helpful, here is a link to the blog on our website about the use of the word rescue: Take off the cape: Why using the word rescue is harmful to anti-trafficking efforts

Anyways, like I said, I think it is great that you are approaching this topic. It is very important. Just wanted to share my thoughts on that particular word:)[2]

ACT: *FIVE*

LEARN

1) Read more on Harmony's perspective on the word "rescue" Take off the cape: Why using the word rescue is harmful to anti-trafficking efforts (3 – 5 mins)

2) Read Love146's Language & Media Guide (5 – 7 mins)

REFLECT

1) Look at rights4girls' #nosuchthing as a child prostitute campaign and the implications for media, legislation, law enforcement, everyday people. (3 – 5 mins)

2) Pay attention to the words you use or hear people using in articles, posts, or legislation related to human trafficking. What do you notice?

everydayaboltionist.co

Share resources, reflections, thoughts or feelings on Chapter 5 or find out what others are thinking or feeling by visiting or commenting at everydayabolitionist.co/book/ch5

Six

FEAR

"The only thing to fear is fear itself."

—*Franklin D. Roosevelt*

I almost didn't write this section.

When it occurred to me that I should include my experience of fear, I was a little . . . afraid.

Afraid to put it out there, to admit it "out loud," on paper. No joke. What would people think? Would I increase the risk of the things I'm afraid of happening? This isn't a movie or a comic book. This is real life with real people who hurt other people who get in the way of their profit.

When I first decided to get more intentionally involved with anti-trafficking efforts, I wasn't that afraid. At the movie screening followed by the panel with the London Metropolitan Police, IJM, Hope for Justice & Sophie Hayes Foundation, someone asked a question about being afraid. I don't even remember the answer the Met Police gave, because, well, I wasn't feeling in the least bit afraid. Hey, this is worth risking being hurt for, I thought.

It wasn't until later that I thought, am I putting the people I care about at risk? You've seen the movies, if you want to hurt someone, you don't hurt them, right? The villain kidnaps or threatens to harm someone they love. That's when I felt afraid.

Then I thought, these fears are probably irrational, similar to being afraid of a shark attack or a plane crash. It's not that the danger doesn't exist, but the fear is out of whack, out of proportion with the likelihood of something ever happening.

It's pretty irrational. I think part of it is that the risk of whatever we fear occurring is out of our control. The only way to be sure is to not go in the ocean and not get on a plane. But the likelihood of dying in a car crash is much greater than in a plane crash. And the likelihood of being bitten by a shark? Statistically, very low.

So then I thought, let's think about this calmly and rationally.

First, harm in the real the world is real, so take appropriate precautions.

Second, a lot of these traffickers wouldn't even be on the same *continent* as me, and the ones that are probably wouldn't benefit from paying any attention to me.

It seems like being afraid of spiders or snakes. The potential harm is legitimate, but "they're more afraid of you than you are of them." I used to work in an unfinished garage. Lots of spiders. But when I walked in and turned on the light, the spiders always retreated into the nooks and crannies. For a rattlesnake, the rattle is a warning to stay away because the snake would really prefer not to bite you. So, let the feeling of fear serve its purpose in helping you be wise and cautious.

I asked two of the people I got to speak with about this, and I don't remember specifically what they said, but it was essentially, "We don't deny there is risk, but we take proper precautions and get on with it." I often think of the people who are boldly involved, people who are way more public and in far more dangerous situations. I'm grateful for their example.

ACT: *SIX*

REFLECT (1 – 5+ mins)

Has fear been preventing you from getting involved in some way? Have you considered whether your fear is irrational?

ACT

Assess the Risk (5 – 10+ mins)

You may be familiar with doing a risk assessment. (If you're a parent of little ones, or of a child of any age, for that matter, you're used to doing this almost constantly! Where are the sharp corners? What's hot? Is there water they could fall into? Who are they going out with tonight?) A written risk assessment is a formalization of that natural process. What are the risks? What's the likelihood of the various risks happening? What are the consequences if one happens? What are steps that can be taken to reduce risk? Then you decide whether or not to do whatever it is you're considering doing.

At worst, a risk assessment can become a mindless or meaningless practice. But if it's a legitimate process to think through the risks and then to decide whether or not to do something, and if so, taking steps to minimize them (such as training or preparation or other precautions), then, it's really helpful in preventing avoidable harm.

Write it down. Writing things on paper can take something out of the realm of irrational fear and into an assessment of real risk. Then, understand the risk. Think about what you can to reduce it. Decide if it's acceptable. Proceed with caution. Don't live in fear.

everydayaboltionist.co

Share resources, reflections, thoughts or feelings on Chapter 6 or find out what others are thinking or feeling by visiting or commenting at everydayabolitionist.co/book/ch6

Seven

FOOLS RUSH IN

(REST & REFLECT)

"You don't think, you react. But, because you didn't think it through, your reaction causes more harm than good down the road."

Rob Morris, Love 146

You may be chomping at the bit, asking, "I thought this was about what I could do? When do we get to that?" And I hope you are. If you care about this issue, as I do, you probably have felt like, "We have to do something about this! And I mean, NOW!"

Real people are suffering terrible abuse, possibly in horrific conditions, right now! We have to act to get them out of those situations. There is real urgency because these are real people experiencing real pain and trauma. Sometimes I had trouble going to sleep thinking about what was happening to someone somewhere in the world.

When we are moved by this issue, we naturally want to do things with urgency. But, as the old song says, fools rush in. And as Rob Morris warns, an unthought "reaction causes more harm than good down the road."[1]

As much as we want to act quickly, it's important to act wisely.

Wax on; wax off, Grasshopper.

And sometimes the slow way is the fast way.

If someone has fallen through the ice, and we rush out to rescue them, but then fall through ourselves, now two people need to be rescued. If someone is in a burning building, and we rush in unprepared, then the first responders will likely have two people they need to rescue, rather than one.

Maybe you'll find yourself in a situation where quick action is needed and appropriate. In that case, you're likely to be more effective if you've taken the appropriate time to prepare well.

Questions include: What happens if things go wrong? What happens if they go right?

If we don't have a plan and take the time to coordinate with others, we could not only be ineffective and inefficient (duplicating what others are already doing, for example), we could actually cause more harm to the victim, the victim's family, or future victims.

One person I met with told me of a well-meaning person who called for advice. The person had been showing up where women were being prostituted and offering the women an opportunity to leave the situation. The person called, both excited and clearly unprepared. "Someone said, yes! . . . What do I do now?"

And what happens if they go unexpectedly? Are you prepared for all of the possibilities for yourself and for the people you're hoping to help? If things go wrong? If things go right? If things don't go as planned? What training do you need? Are there others already working on this? If you succeed, what then? What happens next? To the person? Will another person be trafficked into the same situation to replace them? What now?

Plan for what happens if things go wrong. Plan for what happens if things go right. Plan for a sustainable pace.

"The victims of injustice in our world do not need our spasms of passion; they need our long obedience in the same direction—our legs and lungs of endurance; And we need sturdy stores of joy."

—Gary Haugen, IJM

ACT: *SEVEN*

REST & REFLECT

We've finished Part I! Seems like a good time to pause, rest and reflect.

In Part I, we've focused on preparation, including potential emotions and possible pitfalls.

In Part II, we're going to look at various aspects of addressing modern slavery / human trafficking: prevention, intervention and restoration.

For Chapter 7, there's no additional resource.

Take the opportunity to rest and reflect.

REFLECT

Is there an aspect of human trafficking you notice yourself being concerned or caring about specifically? Do you sense that you care most about a specific area of the world or place? What questions do you have? What training or resources might you need?

everydayaboltionist.co

Share resources, reflections, thoughts or feelings on Chapter 7 or find out what others are thinking or feeling by visiting or commenting at everydayabolitionist.co/book/ch7

PART II

PREVENTION, INTERVENTION & RESTORATION

Eight

HEALTHY SKEPTICISM

(ON NUMBERS)

As I went to buy my daily coffee recently (iced mocha, 2 pumps of mocha, even in the middle of winter), I was standing in line and saw a promotion for bottled water: "Become an instant hero," it beckoned.

Really? I can become a hero instantly? Just like that? And all I have to do is buy a bottle of water? Does that really make me a "hero?"

I'm skeptical.

And when it comes to human trafficking, we should also be a little skeptical.

As I was learning everything I could about human trafficking, I had breakfast with another friend of a friend outside Washington, D.C. (my friends have amazing friends!), John Cotton Richmond, a human trafficking prosecutor and co-founder of The Human Trafficking Institute.

As I was asking questions, listening, and sharing what I had been learning, I casually shared about an initiative I had heard about that had prevented some hundreds of people from being trafficked. He simply said something along the lines of, "When it comes to numbers, be skeptical."

So when I hear numbers claimed about the scope of human trafficking and anti-trafficking, I'm a little cautious. I try to have a healthy skepticism. Ultimately, whether the total number of people enslaved is 45.8 million or 23 million, that's way too many millions too many.

However, it does have implications for resource allocation in addressing the issue. The scope of the issue informs the scope of the response. Therefore, improving estimates is important. It's not easy to get accurate estimates because trafficking is an illegal activity and people hide its occurrence. However, it's not impossible to get good estimates. The Global Slavery Index is one measure which continues working to improve the precision of the figures.

If getting accurate numbers of people enslaved is difficult (though research is growing and getting more accurate), what about anti-trafficking efforts? Here, I think it's helpful to understand overall categories. In anti-trafficking efforts, like other initiatives to address something happening in society, there are three broad categories: prevention, intervention and restoration or "pir," if you will.

There are more specific aspects of anti-trafficking than these, but they broadly fit into one or more of these categories. In reverse order, restoration involves the process of overcoming trauma and of healing. Intervention is being involved in a trafficked person exiting that situation. And prevention is taking action to keep a person from being trafficked in the first place.

Organizations tend to be strong in one area and could "minor" in others. It's difficult, if not impossible, to major in all three at once. Maybe an organization is a "capital" P and "lowercase" i and r, majoring in prevention and less focused on or effective in intervention and restoration. We could describe them as "Pir." Another organization may be pIr and a third is piR. Yet another is exclusively "P." They do not intentionally work on intervention or restoration at all (but they recognize the need to connect, coordinate and/or collaborate with strong I and strong R organizations, as well as with other strong capital P organizations). If we each do what we do best and connect with others in and out of our geography, focus area and specialization, the more effective the anti-trafficking "safety net" will become.

Freedom Collaborative, an online community platform with brings together anti-traffikcing organizations and stakeholders from around the world, states "A networked problem requires a networked solution." I like to say: "The strength of the net is determined by the strength of the knots."

So, when it comes to numbers and modern slavery / human trafficking, have a healthy skepticism. I think this is especially true when it comes to prevention. While "an ounce of prevention is worth a pound of cure," prevention, which is the best scenario because someone never experiences the trauma of being trafficked, is just harder to measure.

Rescue? 24 boys rescued. Check.

Restoration? 17 children participating in art therapy, 41 women employed with a living wage, 5 men in skills training. Check. Check. Check.

Prevention? Harder to measure.

When to comes to prevention, ask: Is that number accurate? How did they measure? Was it estimation?

500 people protected? How do they know? How do I know they know?

Trafficking info booklets were shared with 500 people. Okay.

55 volunteers had 650 conversations with refugees, walking them through how to recognize tactics and avoid being deceived by traffickers. Got it.

365 people now have citizenship papers. Awesome!

37 at-risk girls are somehow specifically being empowered to pursue their dreams. Rad!

1,000 people prevented from being trafficked? Skeptical.

1,673 people called the trafficking hotline, which led to 343 victims assisted and 107 arrests. Gold.

Free 5 slaves for $25? I doubt it.

Become an instant hero . . .? I don't think so.

So, when it comes to numbers, have a healthy skepticism. Assess the source, methodology and motivation. Recognize the nature of trafficking as an illegal activity, where victims may not self-identify as victims. This makes it hard, if not impossible to measure with precision.

ACT: *EIGHT*

LEARN

Learn More About (5 – 15 mins)

A. **Types**: Choose one type of slavery to learn more about via Polaris Project's Modern Slavery Typology

B. **Places**: Choose one of the countries in the Global Slavery Index to learn more about.

C. **Methodology**: Learn about the Global Slavery Index methodology

CONNECT

Connect with others in your area (of interest and/or geography)

Explore:

- Freedom United (freedomunited.org)
- Polaris Project's Global Modern Slavery Directory (globalmodernslavery.org)
- Freedom Collaborative (freedomcollaborative.org)

everydayaboltionist.co

Share resources, reflections, thoughts or feelings on Chapter 8 or find out what others are thinking or feeling by visiting or commenting at everydayabolitionist.co/book/ch8

Nine

WHAT CAUSES TRAFFICKING?

(ON POVERTY AND PUSH & PULL FACTORS)

"No one will find in this volume any argument for reducing our traditional efforts to fight poverty. On the contrary, the billions still mired in fierce poverty cry out for us to redouble our efforts. But one will find in these pages an urgent call to make sure that we are safeguarding the fruits of those efforts from being laid waste by the locusts of predatory violence."

—*Gary Haugen*, The Locust Effect

Doesn't poverty cause trafficking?

As I began seeking ways to make a difference and prevent trafficking happening in the first place, I was talking with some friends and shared my desire to help. They are connected to some fantastic people at a great organization. They said they'd talk to their contacts about what would make a difference.

A few days later, I got an email, which could be summarized, "if you want to prevent trafficking, alleviate poverty." Ok, I thought. That makes sense. Stop poverty; stop trafficking.

But I wondered, does poverty cause trafficking? Is poverty the biggest factor in predicting trafficking? It sounded plausible.

So I set out to find out about the relationship between poverty and trafficking. I took a 500-level course about poverty and development. I studied and wrote my final paper for the course about the relationship between poverty and trafficking. I read everything I could get my hands on: articles, government documents and academic research papers with statistical analysis.

Is there a correlation? And if there is a correlation, does that mean that poverty leads to trafficking (causation)?

I found out, after reading a lot of articles and research papers, when it comes to trafficking, there are multiple risk factors, including poverty. I also learned there are other "push & pull factors" that may combine to make people vulnerable to being caught in clutches of traffickers.

So, this may not make some people happy, but:

If you want to help alleviate poverty, work to alleviate poverty.

If you want to help stop trafficking, work to stop trafficking.

If they overlap, you can be working on both, but don't assume that poverty equals trafficking. Or that poverty alleviation equals anti-trafficking.

It's an oversimplification at best and inaccurate or misleading at worst. Some potential problems with equating the two are the dilution of focus, unintended allocation of resources, or even omitting a specific anti-trafficking focus in various spheres, such as legislation or international agreements and goals.

Poverty is one of many risk factors, and it may not even be the most important risk factor for various groups of people. Other factors such as statelessness (lacking or being denied citizenship), cultural/religious beliefs and/or corruption can be more significant.

Yes, people living in poverty may be at risk.

Yes, we should work to alleviate and eliminate poverty!

But don't equate alleviating poverty with preventing trafficking. They're not exactly the same.

ACT: *NINE*

LEARN (5 – 10 mins)

Read David Feingold's article "Human Trafficking"

NEXT (5 – 10 mins)

Read the section of my final paper (below).

Here's a section of the final paper I wrote for my graduate level class on poverty and trafficking (the professor suggested my section title might not be appropriate for a graduate-level academic paper).

What's Poverty Got to Do, Got to Do With It?

Widespread assumptions commonly identify poverty and lack of education as primary factors in making a person or community susceptible to trafficking, but that is often not the case (Masci, 2004, 4, UNIAP SIREN 2007, 1). The factors involved in trafficking are complex (Masci, 2004, 19). In fact, many studies in Southeast Asia demonstrate that poverty, low levels of education and lack of understanding about human trafficking are *not* necessarily key contributing factors to vulnerability at all (UNIAP 2007, 1, emphasis in original)! In 2005, Feingold, sensing growing misconceptions, wrote to dispel eight myths about human trafficking. One of the myths he cited was that trafficking was "driven by poverty." He dismissed that explanation as "[t]oo simple," and noted that in some parts of Africa girls from mid-sized towns are more at risk than those in more impoverished rural villages (Feingold, 31). A seminal 2001 study on commercial sexual exploitation of children in North America reported that for the majority of children in the study, poverty was *not* the primary factor contributing to their exploitation (Estes & Weiner, 2001, 42). A study of slavery in Silicon Valley, however, found that poverty *is* a risk factor regardless of the type of exploitation and is also a "barrier to victims' long-term recovery" (Not For Sale, 2014, 2).

Cho identifies four categories of factors to capture the diverse potential push and pull factors: migration, crime, vulnerability and policy and institutional efforts (Cho, 3). A statistical study using multiple regression methodology conducted in 2007 by Kevin Bales, a pioneer in research of modern slavery, looked at 76 factors thought potentially predictive of transnational slavery and trafficking and concluded that relevant factors included "corruption, poverty, conflict and the pull-factor of opportunity" (Bales, 2007, 272, 278).

Other factors identified by the International Labor Organization as potential risk factors are being a low- or unskilled worker (ILO, 2014, 6), sudden income shocks to poor households (ILO, 2014, 6), lack of education and literacy (ILO, 2014, 6), and gender—55% of victims are women and girls (ILO, 2014, 8). In commercial sexual exploitation and domestic work the majority are women and girls, in other types of slavery, men and boys are a higher percentage (ILO, 2014, 6).

Migration is also an "important factor" (ILO, 2014, 7). Forty-four percent of people in forced labor had migrated across or within borders (ILO, 2014, 7). Many to most victims of cross-border trafficking become victims because they seek a better life or more economic opportunity (Bales, 2007, 269, Mahmoud, 2). Root causes of slavery include "the greed of criminals, economic pressures, political instability and transition, and social and cultural factors" (Bales, 2007, 269). In some countries, social or cultural practices contribute, such as the devaluation of women and girls and entrusting poor children to wealthier friends or relatives (Bales, 2007, 269). Another study researching cross-border trafficking, which began with 78 push and 67 pull factors, found that crime prevalence "robustly explains" trafficking incidence both in origin and destination countries (Cho, 2012, 1), and gender discrimination and development do *not* have a straightforward correlation with trafficking, and, contrary to expectation, may actually have a limiting effect (Cho, 2012, 3, 1). Clearly this goes beyond attribution to poverty alone.

UNIAP concludes emphatically that poverty does not *cause* slavery/trafficking at all, but rather people who act criminally enslave people (UNIAP). Understanding that poverty does not cause slavery, we can examine evidence regarding the correlation of poverty to slavery. However, it is important to keep in mind that correlation is not causation. While addressing poverty may help, an anti-trafficking initiative which assumes poverty is the primary or significant contributing factor, while doing good and important work to reduce poverty, may not have the desired impact of reducing slavery.

REFERENCES

Bales, Kevin, (2007), *What Predicts Human Trafficking*, *International Journal of Comparative and Applied Criminal Justice*, Fall 2007, 31:2, 269-279

Cho, Seo-Young (2012): *Modeling Determinants of Human Trafficking, Discussion Papers*, Ibero America Institute for Economic Research, No. 216.

Estes, Richard J., & Weiner, Neil A., *Commercial Sexual Exploitation of Children in the U.S., Canada and Mexico*, University of Pennsylvania, Philadelphia, PA., 2001

Feingold, D., Human Trafficking, Foreign Policy, 2005.

ILO, Profits and Poverty: The Economics of Forced Labour Executive Summary, 2014, Geneva, Switzerland.

Masci, D., (2004), "Human Trafficking and Slavery: Are the World's Nations Doing Enough to Stamp It Out?", CQ Researcher, 2004, March.

Omar Mahmoud, Toman; Trebesch, Christoph (2009): The Economic Drivers of Human Trafficking: Micro-Evidence from Five Eastern European Countries., Proceedings of the German Development Economics Conference, Frankfurt a.M., 2009, No. 38.

UNIAP, Human Trafficking Background Information, no-trafficking.org/resources_background_risks.html

UNIAP (2007): Targeting Endemic Vulnerability Factors To Human Trafficking, Bangkok, Thailand.

everydayaboltionist.co

Share resources, reflections, thoughts or feelings on Chapter 9 or find out what others are thinking or feeling by visiting or commenting at everydayabolitionist.co/book/ch9

Ten

LAW & DISORDER

(LAW ENFORCEMENT & JUSTICE SYSTEMS)

"Mom, there's nothing to eat."

Have you ever heard or said that yourself? Depending on your circumstances, it could mean different things. If your children say it while staring blankly into the refrigerator, it translates: "Mom, there's nothing in this half full fridge I feel like eating."

I'm guilty of this as well. I have plenty to eat but there may be nothing I feel like eating. I think about *where* my family's next meal will come from, not *if* we will have one. But for others in the world, "there's nothing to eat" means exactly that. No food, and unsure whether any more will come.

I like watching wilderness survival programs. People are dropped into a variety of harsh environments with little or no gear and tasked with surviving for days or finding their way to civilization. I watch from the warmth of my home and the comfort of my sofa. My refrigerator is at least half full. I have money in my wallet and the supermarket is just down the road.

These TV programs have taught me that two of the first things you have to find are food and water. You can live for 3 days without water and 3 weeks without food. But what else? How long can you live without protection and safety?

Along with strategies for finding food and water, the survivalist assesses potential danger. The threat is often the extreme conditions, a blazing sun or temperatures below freezing, sometimes wild animals. But for many boys and girls, women and men in the world today, the real and immediate threat is other people—people who use violence to rob the poor and vulnerable of their food, shelter, and safety. For victims of trafficking, it doesn't usually start with violence or force, but rather deception, such as an offer of a job in another place, another city, maybe another country, far from the help of family and friends and beyond the reach of trustworthy law enforcement.

A friend of mine was recently burgled while he and his family were home. The burglars brandished weapons as they robbed the house. Thankfully, all were physically unharmed, and it happened in a country where the police are well trained, trustworthy and reliable. They acted swiftly, and the thieves were apprehended.

But what if you called the police and no one came to help you? What if the police *were* the criminals: corrupt or complicit? What if there was no way to get justice if someone harmed you or your children? What if violent criminals in your neighborhood had no fear of being stopped or caught?

For poor people throughout the developing world, the fear of violent criminals acting with no fear of justice is everyday life. Without protection and access to justice, their livelihoods and very lives are never safe and secure.

Instead, the risk of violence can keep children from attending school; it can steal the profit made from hard work; it can steal a person's very body. Injustice can leave an innocent father languishing in jail for months or years for crimes he never committed nor was ever charged with and leave someone enslaved, under the physical or psychological control of a trafficker.

Our daily needs go beyond food, clean water, shelter and medicine. Safety from violence is a basic need without which our efforts to alleviate poverty or stop slavery will be undermined.

ACT: *TEN*

LEARN

Watch a short video (3 mins)

Watch the short video about what IJM founder, Gary Haugen, calls *The Locust Effect* (ijm.org/the-locust-effect)

NEXT

Listen to a Podcast Episode (30 mins)

Listen to Episode 137 of the Ending Human Trafficking podcast: an interview with prosecutors John Cotton Richmond and *The Locust Effect* co-author, Victor Boutros, about their work with The Human Trafficking Institute to decimate trafficking.

everydayaboltionist.co

Share resources, reflections, thoughts or feelings on Chapter 10 or find out what others are thinking or feeling by visiting or commenting at everydayabolitionist.co/book/ch10

Eleven

A VOICE FOR THE VOICELESS?

(ADVOCACY & AGENCY)

Have you signed an online petition before?

I have.

At least twice that I can think of. I'm not sure how I feel about it. Maybe it's because the mental image I have of a petition comes from the scene in the movie *Amazing Grace* where William Wilberforce dramatically drops the scroll of signatures upon signatures, which unrolls along the length of the floor in parliament, from where he stands to the seat of the speaker, in front of all the on looking MPs, as well as the clergy and spectators in the gallery, and then . . . nothing. Nothing becomes of it. No law is passed. Nothing changes. Session suspended.

I know rationally that contributing my signature, electronic or otherwise, communicates something to elected officials, and I'm not saying don't sign a petition. Sometime in the not-too-distant-but-distant-enough future, a law may be passed, funds may be allocated (technical word =

appropriated), a policy might be changed. It doesn't make it unimportant, it's just that's one of the challenges of advocacy.

In some ways, electronically "signing" something just feels too, I don't know, small, or unimportant, or easy. Click. Aaaand, done?

I signed. I even shared. And then I wondered: what difference did that make? Studies show that one of the biggest motivating factors for people to take action is seeing the difference they have made. Did me signing make a difference? How do I know?

There's a theory about social media you may have heard of called "slacktivism." It describes the possibility that clicking, liking and/or following something to do with a social movement on social media actually makes someone *less* likely to do something else about it, whether it's showing up or making a donation or taking another action.

This is akin to setting my Amazon Smile to International Justice Mission (IJM) and thinking that I don't need to give any more money to make a difference. Well, after making some purchases on the old Smile, Amazon informs me that I've generated exactly $6.21 for IJM. While it's not nothing, it sure is not a lot. And if I'm under the impression that, because I've set my Amazon Smile to an anti-trafficking not-for-profit, I've ticked that box and don't need to do anything further to make a difference, I'm sadly mistaken.

(To give due respect to Amazon Smile, it also tells me that my chosen charity, currently IJM, has received $38,317.40 as of this writing, and "All Charities" have received over $46 million. That's awesome. *Amazon* is doing something to make a difference. Well done. The point is that if I think *I've* made all the difference personally by setting up my Smile account, and I can brush my hands off, job done, then I'm being naive.)

I feel the same is true for advocacy. I'm not saying don't sign a petition, and I'm not saying don't write a letter. By all means, sign and write and share. But don't stop there! If you stop there, it could be the advocacy equivalent of giving $6.21. I'm not saying that things have to be difficult to make a difference, or they're only valuable if they're hard to do. I am saying, if you raise your voice, follow up.

Also, understand two different dynamics of advocacy. Advocacy happens at multiple levels, and there are multiple roles you can play, postures you can take.

First, use your voice, not for the voiceless, but on behalf of those whose voice is not being heard. Rarely, if ever, are people voiceless. Maybe their voices aren't being heard. They've been silenced, or maybe no one is listening. Use your ears. Listen because what you think is important may not be what those you want to advocate for find most important.

Know that an advocate can play multiple roles, including speaking for, speaking alongside and supporting someone in speaking for themself. [1] Your most important role as an advocate may be supporting the voice of someone, validating and supporting the agency the person. Agency means the will and ability to act. People trafficked and enslaved aren't voiceless or powerless. However, their power may have been ignored or denied or squelched. In your advocacy, be careful not to accidentally ignore or deny their power, too. When possible, it's often better to support someone in using their voice, acknowledging their agency and personhood in the process.

Second, advocacy happens at multiple levels: International, Regional, National, Local, Community, Family and Interpersonal.[2] Uri Bronfenbrenner, a developmental psychologist, created the Ecological Systems Theory to describe the various spheres of influence on a child's development. They include a microsystem, mesosystem, exosystem and macrosystem, with the child at the center and moving outward from the child. Bronfenbrenner's Ecological Systems Theory can be applied to any individual and gives a framework for the different spheres in which advocacy may be needed. Writing your Prime Minister, President, Chancellor, Senator, Member of Parliament, your state or county representative, the local school authority or speaking up within a community or family, all represent advocacy at different levels.

You may be best placed to serve as an advocate in one or more of these roles on one or more of these levels. Only you, or perhaps those who know you well, can know where and in what role you can be most effective.

And your advocacy may change over time with your location, position, experience or relationships. Issues are constantly changing. So are policies and legislation. Ask, "Does some policy or legislation need to be changed, enacted (or maybe just enforced!), or funded (big word = appropriated)?"

What roles and on what levels are a fit for you now, what can you start doing now that you could continue to grow in and build on over the next months and years?

ACT: *ELEVEN*

REFLECT (5 mins)

Where could adding your voice help? Is it possible you're better positioned and it would be more important to help someone else's (underheard/unlistened to) voice be heard? At what level (i.e. in which of Bronfenbrenner's Ecological Systems)?

ACT

Sign a Petition (1 min)

Find out what's going on now and lend your voice, not to the voiceless, but on behalf of the underheard, the unlistened-to. And then follow up. Stick around. If appropriate, show up in person (lobby). And in the midst, make sure you're using the two ears, one mouth principle: listen twice as much as you speak.

See the current campaigns & sign a petition at:

- Freedom United (freedomunited.org/advocate/)
- IJM's "Freedom Commons:"
  (freedomcommons.ijm.org)

NEXT

Go Further In Depth (1 minute to download; 60+ minutes to read)

Download and read Tearfund's Advocacy Toolkit

everydayaboltionist.co

Share resources, reflections, thoughts or feelings on Chapter 11 or find out what others are thinking or feeling by visiting or commenting at everydayabolitionist.co/book/ch11

Twelve

SUPPLY (CHAINS) & DEMAND (FREEDOM)

*"Sir even you, you have hundred of slaves
whose descendants will curse our names
when we're safe in our graves...
Well, you asked how I feel.
I don't pretend to know the answer,
but the question is real."*

—Lin-Manuel Miranda as Alexander Hamilton,
Cabinet Battle 3 – Demo, Hamilton Mixtape

Icky.

Today, I feel totally icky.

Gross.

Dirty.

Like I want to take a shower and wash away the grime.

Strip naked and put all my clothes in a pile and burn them.

Along with my watch and my sunglasses.

And my shoes.

Just in case.

In case there was any slavery involved in their manufacture.

I've been reading about slavery in supply chains, from chocolate to electronics to apparel and more.

The potential for slavery is all around us.

Like the wooly mammoth pulled over our eyes.

Like the Matrix.

I can hear Morpheus: Slavery is all around you. It could be in the coffee you're sipping, the minerals in the tablet you're reading on, the mobile phone in your pocket, the clothes on your back . . .

I took the survey at slaveryfootprint.org

Evidently, a bunch of slaves work for me.

Stupid red pill.

What am I supposed to do now?

This rabbit hole is staggeringly deep.

Of course I don't want slaves working for me, making the things I wear and use daily.

I don't want to (metaphorically) eat the flesh of a child trafficked into cocoa production in the Ivory Coast.

. . .

Now that I know, I have to say: It's hard to find out whether the products I love are already slave free or whether companies are working to eliminate slavery from their supply chains.

And companies, I believe, don't want slaves working for them either . . . but,

Supply chains are massive, huge and complicated, right?

Companies have to make a profit, right?

Currently, knowthechain.org is good places to start. And I recommend searching for your favorite brand/company there or checking out the "A" ratings in the categories that you often buy or have an upcoming purchase.

I'm feeling good about the Patagonia satchel I sling over my shoulder most days.

And I had the impression that Nike was horrible, but turns out they're listed with a "B" rating (on an A – F scale), so that's above average, just like Adidas.

But what if the company I want to know about isn't listed on knowthechain? Like the running shoes I just bought or the sandals that fit me best?

How does a corporate responsibility statement compare with actual practice? How effective is the supply chain legislation enacted in California or the United Kingdom?

And what do I do with the stuff I already own? Like the sweet raincoat I've had for multiple years whose manufacturer got a "D" from free2work?

And where can I buy slave free running gear or slave free running shoes?!

I'm so overwhelmed I'm actually considering running barefoot. But taking that to it's logical conclusion would have me running *Chariots of Fire* style (the competition scene, not the beach scene) which, although I've lost a stone (14 lbs.) over the past 5 months and the weather is currently a balmy 70 degrees, would probably turn some heads and get me arrested or at least end me up on YouTube.

On second thought, maybe I just need a second Patagonia satchel and some strategic placement.

I actually feel kind of depressed.

Maybe some chocolate will help.

Thank God the chocolate I found in my cupboard is FairTrade.

So what now?!

If companies care about profit more than they care about people, at least they care about profit, right?

So we consumers, the tail end of the supply chain, can vote with our dollars (or pounds or euros, or whatever currency we make our purchases with).

If they won't respond to requests, they will respond to our demand, i.e. consumer demand.

Let's start a buycott!

Reward companies that are already slave-free or are demonstrating progress; stop buying products from companies who aren't making progress.

It's about time for the tail (end of the supply chain) to wag the dog.

Epilogue:

Simple, right?

Not so much.

But, two thoughts are keeping me from being totally overwhelmed right now.

1. I can't unbuy what I have bought, but I can begin buying differently.

2. The Ocean is Made of Drops.

One step at a time, friends. Some small, some substantial, all significant.

Note: This isn't meant as a slam of any particular company. If anything it is an indictment of me, of us, as consumers. But now I've taken the red pill and the illusion I was living in is being removed.

Remember, we are on a journey, to learn and to change, to improve. To make different decisions, to prompt questions, start conversations and inspire informed actions. We don't have all the answers, or maybe even all the questions, but we can commit to progress and increasing informed action. And there are a number of companies, both large and small who are committed to making progress, too.

ACT: *TWELVE*

INTERACT

Take the Survey at slaveryfootprint.org (5 – 10 mins)

LEARN

Got a Mobile Phone?

Watch wetheeconomy's short film: *Supply Chain Reaction* (7 mins)

LEARN

Check out madeinafreeworld.com (5 mins)

Sign up for updates from knowthechain.org (3 mins)

NEXT

Look Into a Related Topic: Demand Reduction— Whether sex trafficking or forced labor, "People don't enslave people to be mean to them. They do it to make a profit." Just like other areas of supply and demand, could reducing the demand for commercial sex and/or pornography, for example, reduce the risk of forced prostitution?

Search: reducing demand for sex trafficking or reducing demand for human trafficking

Or consider the arguments presented in the article "Demand Reduction: Critical Next Step in the Fight Against Sex Trafficking" by Abigail L. Kuzma

ACT

Buying Freeze or Buying Fast

Choose *not* to buy anything or a specific type/category of things for a week or 30 or 40 days.

ACT

Begin to Buy Intentionally (5 – 10 mins)

Pick *one* item you love or buy frequently.

For example:

- coffee/tea
- cotton

- fruit
- leisurewear
- activewear
- t-shirts
- baseball caps
- seafood
- basics
- outerwear
- sporting goods
- outdoor gear
- microchips

Do a quick search on the company that makes it. What do they say in their Corporate Social Responsibility (CSR) statement? Do they comply the California Transparency in Supply Chains Act or UK Modern Slavery Act? What are others saying about their labor practices?

REFLECT

Look for the Leverage (5 mins)

Are you a leader, decision-maker or any part of a small business, large charity, government or education entity, major, minor or local sports program?

I am convinced companies don't want slavery in their supply chains. Many are already taking steps to make changes or are rediscovering ethical production in their founding values.

Large and multinational corporations have the potential to impact tens or hundreds of thousands of workers. They have huge leverage.

Maybe you're a leader, decision-maker or part of a small business, large charity, government or education entity, major, minor or local sports program.

If you have influence in who your vendors are and what products you buy in bulk (like team or staff uniforms, for example), if you're in procurement or you know someone who is, look for the leverage. Your influence or purchasing decision could make the difference for hundreds or thousands of people.

ACT

Buycott – Put your money where your motivation is.

Consider buying from:

- Krochet Kids (krochetkids.org)
- Patagonia (patagonia.com)
- Liminal Apparel (liminal.org.nz or .au)
- Freeset Global (freesetglobal.com)
- Beulah London (beulahlondon.com)

Or other companies committed to ethical supply chains and worker dignity.

ACT

Download the Good On You – Ethical Fashion App (1 min)

everydayabolitionist.co/buycott

For an updated list of suggestions, links to blogs and articles featuring ethical production, companies who are (or are not) committed to progress visit everydayabolitionist.co/buycott

INTERACT

On Social Media? (3 mins)

Check out Fashion Revolution #whomademyclothes ?

And/or

Let people know you're an #everdayabolitionist committed to making ethical purchases

INTERACT

Know of a Good Article, Blog, App or Other Resource?

Share it. (3 mins)

If you're aware of a good resource, such as a blog, article, app, etc., you can share it in the comments on everydayabolitionist.co/buycott or submit it for consideration at everydayabolitionist.co/resources

everydayabolitionist.co

Share resources, reflections, thoughts or feelings on Chapter 12 or find out what others are thinking or feeling by visiting or commenting at everydayabolitionist.co/book/ch12

INTERLUDE

So far in Part II, we have focused on prevention: addressing risk factors, transforming justice systems and reducing demand for goods and services produced with slave labor.

Prevention, prevention, prevention.

Because, as they say, an ounce of prevention is worth a pound of cure.

Prevention is the best-case scenario, right?

If someone never experiences the trauma of slavery/trafficking, they don't need to exit the situation, nor do they need support in the process of restoration.

Four topics in Part II have been devoted to different aspects of prevention.

In the next, we'll talk about intervention and finally restoration. It's not that intervention and restoration are less important, but partly, I have little to no first hand experience of either, and partly, our time is limited.

Both intervention and restoration done well require quality training and time, so for these two topics, we'll just touch on them as starting points.

But first, a quick story.

A SLAVE TO CHOCOLATE

(MAY CONTAIN SLAVES OR TRACES OF SLAVES)

One Saturday afternoon, a boy and girl went to the local market with their family.

"Can we have some sweets?"

"Sure, kids, but take it easy. Don't overdo it."

They ran up to the sweet stall, got in line and craned their necks over and around to see what they might pick out for their treat today. The spread was like a mini-version of Willy Wonka's chocolate factory. They glanced around it to see if there were any purple and green hints of an Oompa Loompa or two hiding about.

When they got up to the counter, they stood on their tiptoes, grabbing the edge to get a better view.

The little girl zeroed in on the chocolate bars.

"What are those numbers?" the boy asked.

"Oh, those?" asked the vendor. "The 70, 80 and 85? Those are percentages: 70%, 80%, 85%."

"Oh, sweet! I've only ever seen numbers like that on dark chocolate. Dark chocolate is my Dad's favorite. I think I'll buy him a bit as well."

"Well, this is kind of like that, but different. It shows what percent is made without the use of slaves."

The little girl furrowed her brow.

"Slaves?" the boy wondered aloud.

"So this one's only made with 15% slaves?" the girl asked.

"You got it! At least 85% slave free. Guaranteed. Pretty good, eh? You want to sample a bit?"

The boy closed his eyes and imagined putting an African boy's finger in his mouth, taking a bite and gnawing on it. He involuntarily gagged a little bit.

Ignoring the offer, the girl tilted her head, scrunched up her face and asked, "Isn't there any way to guarantee 100%?"

"You want 100% slave free chocolate?" the man scoffed.

"Oh, yes, please," the girl beamed, missing the cue in the man's tone of voice, thinking he was about to pull some out from behind the counter. She was ready to pay extra guaranteed slave free chocolate.

"We've got this one that's an unknown percentage. It might be slave free," the man offered, handing them each a chocolate bar.

The boy looked at the packaging, turning it over in his hands. There was something that looked like an allergy-warning label: May Contain Slaves or Traces of Slaves.

That sounded gross. He shuddered, shook his head and tried to get the image out of his mind.

"These might be slave free. That's the best I can do." The man held a hand out over the counter, palm open, waiting for them to pay for the chocolate bars.

The girl's eyes moved up and to the left, not really looking at anything in particular. She put her hand under her chin, tapping her index finger on her lips. She looked down at the chocolate bar in her other hand. Then, her eyes started darting back and forth as she began thinking out loud.

"Well, if I were allergic to nuts," she began, "and you offered me chocolate that may or may not contain nuts, even just a little, then I'd have to pass because I might have a really bad reaction. I might get really sick or even die. And I think," she paused, her eyes narrowing as she focused and looked the man straight in the eyes, "if you can't guarantee no slaves were used to make this chocolate, there's no way I'm eating it." With her final words she put the chocolate bar back in the man's outstretched hand, with a little more force than she intended.

"Yeah," the boy chimed in, tossing the bar onto the counter, "Even though I'd love to have some right now and to share some with my dad. We're gonna have to pass, because somewhere a boy just like me might be a slave, and might be mistreated or die . . . so I can eat chocolate? I just can't take that risk."

"Kid, what's it to you if some other kid . . . on the other side of the world . . . might . . . and I stress *might* be a slave?"

The man's voice faded away as the boy and girl dodged through the people meandering through the market. When they got back to their parents, they just about knocked them off balance, hugging them around their hips and waists.

"We don't want any sweets from that man today!"

Surprised, the parents said, "Okay, that's a bit strange," and "What happened?"

The siblings looked at each other and then back at their parents.

"It's kind of creepy. We'll tell you. But, first, let's get outta here."

***

Okay. That's a bit morbid, but it's along the lines of what one boy enslaved in Cote D'Ivoire said in the documentary *Slavery: A Global Investigation.*

"They're eating my flesh."[1]

Metaphorically, of course.

I can't help but think of some grotesque Halloween scene.

So what can we do?

ACT: *CHOCOLATE*

LEARN

Find out more about the debate and what the chocolate companies are or are not doing to eliminate slavery from their chocolate.

Read the article: Lawsuit: Your Candy Bar Was Made By Child Slaves (10 mins)

Watch the documentary Slavery: A Global Investigation (80 mins)

Read about slavefreechocolate.org (15 mins)

ACT

Read the packaging.

Look for single source, Fairtrade, organic or Rainforest Alliance certified chocolate.

(Even though organic and Rainforest Alliance aren't certifying slavery free, because there is a certification process and, therefore, external inspection, these benefit from "positive externalities" (an economics term meaning additional benefits to others as a result of one's actions), i.e. the certifiers may not be looking primarily for slavery, but they are looking at how the cocoa beans are sourced and, therefore, would likely see labor conditions and labor practices.)

everydayabolitionist.co

Get a pdf of *A Slave to Chocolate: May Contain Slaves or Traces of Slaves*, share resources, reflections, thoughts or feelings on the story or find out what others are thinking or feeling by visiting or commenting at everydayabolitionist.co/chocolate

Thirteen

TO THE RESCUE?

(A PERSON, NOT A PROJECT: ON INTERVENTION & RESILIENCE)

Intervention can be dramatic. It can make for a good and inspiring storyline, whether TV crime dramas or real life rescue. There is emotional tension, unknown . . . will the heroes succeed? In time? And there's a sense of relief: victims freed, perpetrators caught. It's what stories are made of. If there's no unknown, no uncertainty, no drama, there's no interest. It's why I can't watch a sporting event I've recorded if someone spills the result. It's why we warn of "spoiler alerts." It's why secret agent and superhero movies don't show the hours and hours it takes to travel from one city to another. Boring. And it would take too long.

Actually, intervention done well involves a lot of long and boring, too.

Planning, preparation, waiting, only for a mole to tip off the trafficker; disappointment, more planning, coordination, research, waiting, evidence gathering, maybe another insider tipping off the perpetrator, preventing real people from being removed from slavery. Preparation for things going wrong, preparation for things going right, planning for safety and support of the victims, putting appropriate measures in place to secure the criminals. More disappointment, more drudgery.

Then finally, the day, the hour, the moment, the rescue! Freeeeeeeedom! A silent (or not-so-silent) spike the ball, end zone dance, goal-scorer celebration. And . . . the . . . crowd . . . goes . . . wiiiiiiiiild! And we do. Fired up fist pumps, heartfelt high fives, group hugs with semi-strangers, likes and loves in the hundreds or thousands, a veritable explosion of emoji. This is what we came for.

Yes! Let's rejoice for every rescue! But let's not be naive about everything that goes into it or focus too much on the dramatic moment itself nor be so naïve to think that intervention is defined by or limited to dramatic rescues. Intervention may be one event, or a series of events. There's a lot of preparation before and, I imagine, a lot of paperwork after, not to mention the processes of restoration and pursuing justice. Maybe it's like being a midwife or ob-gyn, the birth is only one event on a certain day. There were a lot of things that happened before, and there'll be a lot to take care of after the baby arrives. Of course we rejoice and celebrate emergence into new life, but in many senses, it is one milestone on a freedom journey.

And the reality is, I'm probably not going to be involved in an intervention. Maybe you will be. If so, I'd think you would want to make sure you get the proper training. Planning for what happens if things go wrong. Planning for what happens if things go right. More likely, when it comes to intervention, you or I might be in a certain place at a certain time, where we recognize the signs and make the phone call.

And that's the training we need. Maybe you're a trucker, a first responder, a flight attendant, or you work at a hotel or a parcel delivery service, or you're an everyday person going about your everyday business. You can be prepared to recognize the signs & make the call. And then get the people with the right training to involved. Like a director calling, "Aaand . . . action!" We're not the star. We're not the hero, but we recognize when the scene is set, and we're ready to roll camera.

Another word about the word rescue. I'm okay with it, depending on the context. If I was in a situation like that, I wouldn't much care what you called it if you helped me get out of the situation. If I fell through the ice and you rescued me, I wouldn't take that to mean I was powerless or helpless, only that I needed help to get out of a situation I couldn't get out of by myself. Calling it a rescue shouldn't imply that someone is powerless. They're not. It may be their power has been diminished, or their power isn't as great as those who control or restrict their power.

Like Harmony said, though, often the word isn't helpful. And, because I'm committed to learning, and I try to be open to other opinions and perspectives, I'm really thinking about what I think about the word rescue.

Whatever your decision on when and if to use the word rescue, I can only imagine the pain, physical and psychological, people in these circumstances endure. And that convinces me that they are definitely not powerless. They are resilient. Not powerless, not voiceless. Resilient.

And you might just be the person, someplace, sometime, in a position, not necessarily to intervene yourself, but to recognize the signs and to both know what to do and what not to do.

ACT: *THIRTEEN*

PREPARE

Be ready to Recognize the Signs. (3 mins each)

Watch this short video by MSP "Look Again"

Read the quick summary "Recognize the Signs" by Polaris Project

ACT

Put Hotline Numbers in Your Mobile (2 mins)

In the USA?

Put these numbers in your mobile phone:

USA National Trafficking Hotline: 1 (888) 373-7888
USA Polaris BeFree Textline: Text "BeFree" (233733)

Be ready to make the call or send the text.

In the UK?

If you have information about modern slavery crimes or where victims may be at risk that requires an immediate response, call the police on 999

Modern Slavery Helpline: 08000 121 700

Or check to see if 0800 555 111 is still valid for making anonymous calls to Crimestoppers

Not in the USA or UK?

Find out if there is a Trafficking Hotline or text number in your country.

Put it in your mobile.

NEXT

Find Out about Training (5 – 10 mins)

Do a quick search for online or in person training relevant to your role or industry, such as:

- **Truckers Against Trafficking** – truckersagainsttrafficking.org
- Hospitality or Security? Start with **Guardian Group** – theguardiangroup.org
- **Airline Ambassadors** – airlineamb.org

- Community leader? Take a look at **i-5 Freedom Network** – i5freedomnetwork.org
- Business leader? Check out **Businesses Ending Slavery and Trafficking (BEST)** – bestalliance.org

Find out if there is anti-human trafficking training available for your profession or in your area. If there isn't, maybe you could help source or coordinating training for your industry or location.

If you're aware of a good training option, you can share it in the comments on everydayabolitionist.co/training or submit it for consideration at everydayabolitionist.co/resources

everydayabolitionist.co

Share resources, reflections, thoughts or feelings on Chapter 13 or find out what others are thinking or feeling by visiting or commenting at everydayabolitionist.co/book/ch13

Fourteen

THE RAIN FOREST

(ON RESTORATION)

What do the Amazon rain forest and human trafficking have in common?

Am I just seeing everything in relation to modern slavery these days?

It's topic fourteen, the final topic in Part II of *Everyday Abolitionist*. Can you believe it?

Has the reality of human trafficking become the lens through which you see the world?

I watched a program on the BBC about a wildlife photographer who buys 100 acres of Amazonian rain forest in Peru.[1] He wants to do his bit for the environment. He comes to realize it's not so simple and straightforward as, "I'll just buy some rain forest and that'll be that."

It's complicated. At one point, he says, "I'm pretty sure I have no idea exactly what I'm getting myself into." And I don't think I do either. But I know I have to do something.

Then he goes to visit a non-profit nearby which has been working to restore deforested areas. They set up cameras on trails and at a salt lick. When they go back to check them, they find pictures of all kinds of wildlife: birds, boar, jaguar. Lots of life! The plant life and the animal life are thriving where once it had been destroyed.

He left with hope. Hope because he had seen restoration is possible. He saw secondary forest can have vibrant life. One cannot turn back the clock and restore primary forest. But with love, care and time, a new secondary forest with vibrant life can grow.

For me, this what I imagine restoration is like. It is the picture I have in my mind as I see the work of organizations like HUG Project, Love 146, Restore NYC, Saving Innocence, Hope For Justice, YouCanFreeUs, and the direct services provided by the Center for Combating Human Trafficking, to name a few.

Like intervention, my involvement with restoration is likely to be indirect. I don't have the specialized skills and training for some aspects of it. You may be inclined toward this area of anti-trafficking work, and if so, there are some fantastic organizations you can support or volunteer with or even work for full time. And there are different aspects to this work as well, such as art therapy, skills training, counseling and providing safe employment.

And if, at some point you think, "Is restoration from such destruction even possible?"

Remember the rainforest. And in time, lots and lots of life!

ACT: *FOURTEEN*

LEARN

Check out these examples (3 – 5 mins each)

Business/Employment: Not For Sale – Dignita Restaurant

Art Therapy: Talitha

Direct Services: Wichita State University's Center for Combatting Human Trafficking (combatinghumantrafficking.org)

ACT

Consider getting involved with:

- HUG Project Thailand (hugproject.org)
- Love 146 (love146.com)
- Restore NYC (restorenyc.org)
- Saving Innocence (savinginnocence.org)
- Hope for Justice (hopeforjustice.org)
- YouCanFreeUs (youcanfree.us)

Or another organization you've heard of!

Especially an organization with a local focus.

NEXT

If this is an area of interest, find out what opportunities there are for you to help directly or indirectly or get the training you need to be involved.

ACT (3 – 10 mins)

Buy something from a company with a specific focus on employing survivors, for example:

- Sudara (sudara.org)
- Aruna (arunaproject.com)
- Sutisana (sutisana.com)
- Purpose Jewelry (purposejewelry.org)
- The Tote Project (thetoteproject.com)
- Nomi Network (nominetwork.org)

RESOURCE

Consider the counseling resource: FAAST Hands That Heal (1 min to download, 60+ to read)

everydayabolitionist.co

Share resources, reflections, thoughts or feelings on Chapter 14 or find out what others are thinking or feeling by visiting or commenting at everydayabolitionist.co/book/ch14

PART III

FREEDOM FORWARD

Fifteen

WE SEE THE SAME SKY

(ON MUTUALITY)

*"If you have come here to help me,
you are wasting your time. But if you have
come because your liberation is bound up
with mine, then let us work together."*

—*attributed to Lilla Watson,
aboriginal Australian leader*

I don't know about you, but I feel like we've hiked a mountain or climbed at least 14 flights of stairs so far. I'm looking out over a horizon (metaphorically). Maybe you are, too. Maybe yours is a landscape or a seascape or a cityscape.

At the same time, I feel like we've gotten down into the nitty, gritty, street-level, gut-level stuff, we've gotten honest and real.

In reality, as I write this, I'm in a coffee shop.

I wonder where you are. Literally? Emotionally?

Wherever in the world you are, if you can, pause and look up. Look around. Look out your window or down the street, along the footpath.

What do you see? *Who* do you see?

Above whoever and whatever's right in front of you is the sky.

Maybe you can see it at the horizon, or directly above you, or maybe it's hidden from view.

As you know, whether it's across an ocean and or around the corner, or likely both, the harsh reality is people are trafficked and enslaved. And appearances can be deceiving. They may or may not appear trapped. They almost definitely will not be in literal chains.

There is a chance they're locked up in a basement, this real human being. There have definitely been instances of that. More likely, though, this person, this woman, man, boy or girl is being manipulated, coerced and controlled in some other way. You might even see them coming or going or through a window somewhere. At first, you might not give them a second glance.

It's been said that we see what we're looking for. Like when you like a certain sports team or a brand of clothing, and you start noticing, Hey, he's repping that logo; she's wearing that brand. Or when you're thinking about buying a certain kind of car and, all of a sudden, you start seeing that type of car in all kinds of places. You start noticing it.

We don't want to mistakenly see slavery where its not. We do want to keep our eyes peeled.

All of us, particularly people like truck drivers, mail carriers, household repair, flight attendants and others can be in places where trafficking might be happening, particularly with the rise of different types of package delivery, or peer-to-peer sales sites. Whether it's in our neighborhood, in a restaurant, a dodgy or not-so-dodgy looking place of business, we need eyes that can recognize signs of trafficking and know what to do and who to call.

Because, people free people.

I'm a person. You're a person. They're a person, too.

Surviving. Strong. Resilient.

Not helpless, but in need of help.

Just like you. Just like me.

There are no self-made people.

No one is an island.

So, in the words of someone from possibly the biggest island in the world, "*[i]f you have come because your liberation is bound up with mine, then let us work together.*"

Wherever we are, whatever we've seen, whatever we see when we look around us, whatever the circumstances we find ourselves in, if we look up, we see the same sky.[1]

Sixteen

A FREEDOM TAPESTRY

(ON INTERCONNECTEDNESS)

"Slavery is too big a problem to solve as individuals."

—*Kevin Bales*, Disposable People

As you contemplate the sky, your surroundings, the people around you, in your life, or reflect on what you've learned, I want to say thanks so much for giving me the privilege of sharing some of my journey with you.

I hope you've learned something, disagreed with me about something, reflected, been encouraged, challenged, empowered and taken meaningful action, some specific steps to move from human trafficking awareness to informed action to stop some specific slavery.

If you've read through quickly, you may want to go back and do some of the suggested actions. When you take some actions, I would love to hear a little about what you've done. Either way, congratulations for reaching this milestone on your journey.

Whew. High fives!

I know it might not have been easy for you for one reason or another.

Hopefully, at the very least, you can be sure you're not alone.

And you shouldn't be alone in this.

You can't do it by yourself. Neither can I. We need each other.

No one can do everything, but everyone can do something.

Individuals, networks, communities, organizations, and on an even higher level, sectors.

Recently, toward the end of the Asia-Region Anti-Trafficking Conference in Bangkok, I was talking with Helen Sworn, Founder of Chab Dai and co-founder of the conference. When I commented on the wide variety of organizations represented, from multi-national corporations to grassroots non-profits to regional and international government to small businesses. Helen said something I think is vital, "I used to say, 'No one organization can address human trafficking.' Now, I'm convinced, no one sector can."[1]

To turn the tide on trafficking, we need not just the non-profit sector or the legal sector or law enforcement or justice systems or governments. We also need corporations and universities, faith communities, civic groups, news and media, international aid and development, the transportation industry and the fashion industry, established institutions and social enterprises, small businesses and Silicon Valley start ups, angel investors and educators, digital natives and digital nomads, stay at home dads and mompreneurs, single people and single parents, billionaires, bikers and bankers, indie artists and entertainment moguls, feminists, philanthropists and freelancers, vegans and vloggers, poets, priests and politicians, grassroots workers and musicians, ragamuffins and royalty, truckers, teachers, ten-year olds and tattoo artists, survivors and scholars and scholar-survivors, second-cousins-twice-removed, teens, tweens and great-grandparents . . . and everyone in between, including you and me, no matter our age, background or bias, becoming an international, interpersonal, interconnected society of everyday abolitionists.

I'm picturing a tapestry. A huge one like they hang on massive walls in castles.

A tapestry is both beautiful and functional. It provides warmth and tells a story. It's made by weaving together different threads in different directions, threads dyed in different colors, interwoven to depict a scene.

In ancient times, the most expensive thread was dyed purple, Tyrian purple. Purple clothing was worn by royalty. It was extremely rare and extremely valuable.

Among other things, purple is also associated with hurt, bruising. Maybe one of the reasons the awareness ribbon for Violence Against Women is purple. It may be associated with being vulnerable. The basis for Tyrian purple dye comes from a sea snail which excretes it when it's attacked or physically antagonized by humans . . . or crushed.

Maybe you've been crushed by the realities of trafficking, either first hand or vicariously. You are vulnerable and valuable. Those at risk of or affected by trafficking are vulnerable and valuable, too. And perhaps crushed as well. But that doesn't have to be the end of their story or yours, we can be woven together in a beautiful, meaningful freedom tapestry.

The question is: Are we going to let our current position, our past, our privilege, or our pain prevent us from participating in the possibility of someone else's freedom? Whatever our past, whatever our place, we need each other.

Let's work together for freedom for every person on the planet.

Together for freedom.

Seventeen

THE TRUCKER, THE TEACHER, THE TEN-YEAR OLD AND THE TATTOO ARTIST

"Each voice matters and every small action counts—whatever your age or your background."

—Rasha Hammad, Youth Underground

What's your part to play in anti-trafficking at this point in your life?

Are you a dentist, tattoo artist or accountant? Can you offer free dental work, tattoo removal and cover-ups or do the books pro bono?

What I'm saying is:

No one can do everything, but everyone can do something.

What *can* you do?

I remember hearing about the Walk Free Foundation's start. An Australian teenager saw modern slavery on a trip, and what did she do? She talked to her dad, an Australian billionaire. Now, in a way, that discourages me. If I'm not a billionaire, which I'm not, and my parent's not a billionaire (nope), does that mean I can't do anything? That I shouldn't bother? No! This is an example of doing what you can do. This girl couldn't do certain things herself, but she knew someone she could influence. So that is what she did.

We are all limited and, by definition, there are things you can't do. Even the billionaire's not the president or the Pope, for example. But you might be in a position to influence someone with the power or position to do something they are in direct control of, and that is doing something.

So, what *can* you do? Who *do* you know?

What about the group of ten-year olds who wrote to the Prime Minister of Great Britain? Or what about the person who asks for donations to an anti-trafficking organization for their birthday instead of presents? Or the one who writes a research paper on Harriet Tubman, William Wilberforce, Frederick Douglass or Olaudah Equiano, or about the Underground Railroad or child slavery on fishing boats on Lake Volta? Or the child who asks his/her parent what they could do as a family to help stop slavery?

The answer to the question, "What can I do today to move freedom forward?" is the bull's-eye in the center of a three-ring target.

Picture this: a trucker, a teacher, a ten-year old and a tattoo artist are playing darts.

Their dartboard has a red bull's-eye in the center, a white inner ring around that, and a red outer ring.

- Red Bull's-Eye = Directly Choose/Change—your decision or action makes a difference
- White Ring = Indirect Influence—your influence could affect someone else's choice or action that makes a difference
- Red Outer Ring = Can't Currently Influence—not currently within your power to do or to influence, but maybe someday in the future

Where are you gonna aim your darts?

Where do you think you could make the biggest difference? Maybe talk to some people about what you're thinking.

If you're the daughter of a billionaire, your most important focus might be the White Ring of Influence!

And, hey, it's important to recognize what you're in position to do might look very different in a different season of life!

Right now, you might need to study, train, research or volunteer. Or maybe you've got three kids under five years old and you don't have time to use the bathroom by yourself.

Then, someday, or next year, what used to be in the red outer ring of "Currently Beyond Your Influence," might move into the white inner ring of "Indirectly Influence" or even into the bull's-eye of "Directly Change!"

Right now, for example, I can choose what I buy (a.k.a. buycott). I can influence (i.e. invite) people to learn, to get involved, take action or give. I can advocate.

There are also some things I can't influence at all . . . yet. Maybe that one should be called the Red Ring of Courage because I need to have courage to take steps to be in position, whether it's next week or next decade (even if it's never!), to make the invitation, make the call, ask, take action and reach out and beyond my current ability to do or influence.

Right now there are a lot of things in the Red Ring of Courage, but there are also a lot in the White Ring of Influence, and right in the Red Bull's-Eye that I can do today.

- What can you do?
- Who can you influence?
- What can't you do or influence currently (but care about and hope to be able to someday)?

Take into account what you can do with one or more other people.

Then, pick one to do next.

And, take the next step and the next one.

If you're listening to the audio version or driving or doing something else that would make this impractical or unsafe, don't do this right now. Do it the next time it's safe to do. Pull out a piece of paper or pull up a note taking app, and write what comes to mind in those three categories, the three rings on the *Everyday Abolitionist* dartboard.

What's in your:

- Red Bull's-Eye of Directly Choose/Change
- White Ring of Influence
- Red Ring of Courage

Are you a trucker, a teacher, a ten year old or a tattoo artist?

Someone else?

I guaran-dog-tee you, no matter who you are 1) there's something you can do now, 2) there's someone you can influence, and 3) there's something you can grow into.

Eighteen

AS EASY AS XYZ
(FIND YOUR FOCUS)

Okay, you've thought a little about what you can do, who and what you can influence and what you might like to do/influence in the future.

Now, take some time to explore *where* you want to concentrate your efforts. For now at least. It isn't set in stone. It's a place to focus so you can get started. Let's call it your starting place.

Of course, I care about all people in all types of slavery everywhere. But I can't help everyone everywhere. My efforts would be spread too thin. They wouldn't make a very big difference.

You may know there's a principle of physics where an amount of force applied over a large area may hardly have any effect, but the same amount of force focused on a small area has a much greater impact, even breaking through the object.

(Hey, breaking through. Breakthrough!)

So, I encourage you to begin or continue to find your focus.

Is there something on your heart? Have you noticed anything particularly making you angry or sad?

If I asked you right now, what would you say?

Right now, I care most about:

X aspect (maybe something we covered, an aspect of prevention, intervention, restoration) of Y type of slavery (if needed, see Polaris Project's Modern Slavery Typology) in Z location.

The more specific the better.

Here it is with blanks:

Right now, I care most about _____ (X = aspect of anti-trafficking) of _____ (Y = type of slavery) in _____ (Z = location).

If you can't fill in all the blanks, fill in the one or two you can.

Again, it may help to look at Polaris Project's Modern Slavery Typology. Or to reflect on what you've thought or felt. Or to talk to some people you know and trust.

Then, take one next step.

A university student did some research for a class and found the most beneficial thing you could do may not be getting on a plane to go to another country. It might be setting up a monthly donation to an organization you resonate with.[1] One idea could be, start to give $15, $50 or $500 a month to an anti-trafficking organization that has your XYZ as their focus.

Pick an amount that is meaningful for you. Set up the monthly donation to an organization you believe in. Make that your down payment. Your ante up. Your pledge. Your promise to learn and connect and take further action.

Whatever you decide to do, what you do next might just mean the difference between slavery and freedom for someone! A real-life, flesh and blood and feelings, human being.

What if your next steps meant someone else's next steps were taken in freedom?

Nineteen

RAISE FREEDOM

I would not do this just for me
Running here so effortly
I would not would not in the rain
Out in this chill grey dark and pain
But, today, I'm here by choice
Persisting now for one child's voice
Today, I run for one small girl
Believing she is worth the world

Speaking of next steps, as I was taking figurative steps on my journey to help in anti-slavery/anti-trafficking, but felt like I wasn't "getting anywhere," like applying for a few jobs and not even getting my application acknowledged, or beginning to dig deeper (which I now see was crucial preparation), but not sure what exactly to do yet. Asking myself: Should I keep applying for jobs in this sector? Volunteer with existing charities? Start a blog? Get an MBA and work in a corporate setting in Corporate Social Responsibility or supply chain management? Work in an "unrelated" field and focus on anti-trafficking outside of work? (I put unrelated in quotes because every job/role/industry has influence and impact on whether slavery is has an environment in which to thrive or is disrupted.) All of these and more are legitimate pathways to make a difference. I just wasn't sure which pathway was the best fit for me.

In 2014, during the first Freecember, I wrote:

> *So at various times over the course of this past decade or more, I have been both heartbroken and outraged, and more recently I have been pursuing ways to be meaningfully involved in helping end modern slavery, human trafficking and violence against the poor. I have been looking for what is a fit for my capacities, abilities, experience and heart . . .*

The next year, I gave a little update:

> *I honestly couldn't figure out what I could do to make a difference, and I wasn't sure what to do about everything I was feeling. I didn't know what I didn't know, and I didn't know what would actually help. I set out to learn as much as I could about human trafficking, and started, or really, continued on a journey, figuratively and sometimes literally. I wrote down but didn't share publicly about what I was learning and thinking and feeling. Then, after talking and dreaming and kicking ideas around with a few friends, and not really knowing what else to do at the time, but wanting to do something, I decided I'd start by trying to go 100 miles in a month and seeing if anyone would be crazy enough to join me.*
>
> *Plus, nothing about slavery is funny. Me exercising . . . Now that has potential.*

That was a few years ago now. The first year, three days before December 1st, I shared with my small social media circles what I was about to attempt: to run/walk 100 miles during what I was calling "Freecember." (I hadn't been running much at the time. And by much, I mean, at all. And by at the time, I mean, since who knows when.) I decided to make my 100 mile challenge all outdoors. (I pretty much hate treadmills.) When I shared, I invited people to join me (virtually or in person if they could). Fairly quickly, I realized I wasn't going to make it 100 miles in a month on foot (100 miles in a month averages to about 5k a day), so two friends let me borrow their bikes and sometimes joined me for rides.

On three days notice, we ended up finishing the first Freecember with these stats:

> Continents: 3
> Languages: 1
> Teams: 1
> People: 18+
> 100 Milers: 7
> Miles: 1,522
> Charities Supported: 5 – IJM, IJM (UK), A21 (AUS), International Sanctuary, Saving Innocence
> Currencies: 3.50 (USD, GBP & AUD – the .50 was for 50 Euro cents that snuck in)
> Monies raised: $2,048

That's how Freecember started. I made it up. Last minute. Totally winged it. People did all kinds of things, not just distance challenges, and they picked the charities they wanted to raise money for. It could be any anti-slavery/anti-trafficking charity anywhere in the world. (You can find out more about how Freecember works at freecember.org)

On Day 4 of the first Freecember challenge, as I biked in the cold drizzle, I thought about the reason why I was run/walk/biking 100 miles: "she's 6 years old, lives in South-East Asia and survived slavery. I haven't met her and don't know her name, but there are caring people from IJM walking with her who have and do," I wrote when I got home. While I was riding, I "thought" a poem. (I made up a word: effortly. It's the opposite of effortlessly.) Here's the poem:

> I would not do this just for me
> Biking here so effortly
> I would not would not in the rain
> Out in this chill grey dark and pain
> But, today, I'm here by choice
> Persisting now for one child's voice
> Today, I ride for one small girl
> Believing she can change the world

As I thought the final lines, I wept.

Right there on my borrowed bike.

Tears and raindrops mingling as they ran down my cheeks.

Over the past few years, as I was running, biking or walking, by myself, with friends or with my kids, I've thought and processed and dreamed and prayed and reflected and chatted and taken selfies and thought poetry and stories and posts and possibilities and helped people raise over $25,000 for a few frontlines organizations.

For a grassroots organization, a little funding can make a big difference.

And since I first started Freecember, people have told me about or I've come across others making a big (or even bigger!) difference raising funds. Runners, walkers and run hosts with Aruna Runs raise awareness, funds and help provide employment opportunities for women. Songs Against Slavery empowers and inspires communities to join the fight against sex trafficking through benefit concerts and musician partnerships. Ping Pong-a-thon recently raised $500,000 and Dressember raised $2 million, with an "M," to fund the frontlines of freedom! Love, love, love and celebrate these!!!

I share this because raising funds is something specific you can do now, no matter who or where you are, and because, whether we raise a little or thousands, when we join together we can raise even more funds for and awareness of amazing, difference making, frontlines organizations.

One year a teenager, who's an ice hockey goalie, raised $2,500 on the nose stopping hockey pucks to stop slavery (sometimes with his facemask).

Recently, a small group of people who believe in the grassroots, frontlines work of WMFBolivia and HUG Project raised $7,820 and over $10,000 for them respectively. I ran 5k a day, every day, for 31 days to represent and raise money to help provide a lunch program for 31 women's children who are in WMFBolivia's weekly program. Another family's kids drew pictures on the theme of freedom and joy every day of Freecember. That family raised $2,075 for HUG Project and created hopeful and inspiring art along the way.

The best pledge to Freecember so far, though, IMO, comes from a mom, who wrote me this:

> Speaking of talking to friends over coffee, my 6 year old, who is doing the "read as much as you can for this month" challenge, was telling her friend at an event about what she was doing. Her friend decided to donate 10 cents for every book she reads :) And now her friend is going to read and see if she can get pledges too! Pretty sweet.[1]

Best. 10 cents. Ever.

Reading about her 6 year old and her friend, I seriously put my arms up like I finished a race or just won something!

Those 10 cents per book are my favorite money raised for Freecember so far!

And it shows me, no matter who we are, we can all do something to help people live in freedom.

I started calling the people joining in Freedom Raisers, because in a very real sense, that's what they're doing, funding the frontlines of anti-slavery and raising freedom levels for real people. Leveling up freedom.

You can become a Freedom Raiser, too! Whether you're six or 106.

Running, walking, wearing a dress, drawing, stopping hockey pucks, reading or playing Ping-Pong might not seem like "doing something" to stop slavery, but when you do what you can, and you do it for a reason and share why you're doing it, these everyday activities can become powerful little BIG difference makers.

ACT: *NINETEEN*

ACT

Become a Freedom Raiser!

Join in and raise funds and freedom:

- Freecember (freecember.org)
- Aruna Runs (arunaproject.com)
- Songs Against Slavery (songsagainstslavery.org)
- Dressember (dressember.org)
- Ping Pong-a-thon (pingpongathon.com)

DIGNITY & DELIGHT

(TO BE CONTINUED . . .)

There's something I want you to know as we wrap up this part of our journey.

I want you to hear it from me because I think it may be a game changer, and it's something that took me a really, really long time to realize. A bit of an epilogue at the end of my initial journey.

See, at first, and for a long time, I thought, how can I enjoy life . . . enjoy *anything* when people are trafficked and enslaved, in horrific situations suffering horrific abuse?

Sometimes I couldn't sleep.

Eventually, what I realized is this:

What I want for every person enslaved is for them to experience dignity and delight, to enjoy life. And that helped me be okay with enjoying life, too, despite whatever reality I wish were different.

And we need to celebrate progress along the way, which is one reason I started Freedom Fortnight (that's British

English for "two weeks")—14 days of focus on anti-trafficking, celebrating progress and innovation in anti-trafficking and highlighting practical ways for people to get involved (freedomfortnight.org).

Freedom Fortnight might be a good next step for you. Or Freecember (freecember.org).

Either could be something you invite some friends to join you in.

Whatever you choose to do next, whatever your epilogue to this part of your journey, keep stepping. Ask questions. Have conversations. Take informed action. Learn and grow. Who knows what you'll get up to?! You might find this epilogue actually becomes your prologue.

And, if you haven't already, get connected.

You can search for local groups or virtual groups. Check out Polaris Project's Global Modern Slavery Directory or Freedom Collaborative (for the intermediate to advanced) or maybe we should start the Everyday Abolitionist Society (which doesn't exist as of this writing!).

The simplest way for you to get started right now may be to sign up on Freedom United (freedomunited.org). I have. You'll be joining in an action oriented global community whose mission is to "INSPIRE millions of people to become lifelong abolitionists, then MOBILIZE them to INFLUENCE governments, business and society to make the changes necessary to end modern slavery."[1]

Or maybe it's starting to or continuing to meet up regularly with friends.

Whatever it looks like for you, find some community. Don't do this alone. If you don't hear anything else from this whole book, whatever you do, don't go alone. The Lone Ranger, Indiana Jones, Lara Croft, Han Solo, they're fiction. Connect with a Band of Brothers and Sisters. Work together to stop some specific slavery.

Finally, as a kind of formal way to mark the end of this leg of our journey together, let me encourage you with the words my best friend spoke to me one of the last times we were together in person:

Pursue your heart for justice.

And this day and to the end of your days, may you live and empower others to live in freedom, with dignity and delight.

To Be Continued . . .

NEXT STEPS

Make Your Mark

In the past (and sometimes today), people enslaved were unable to read and write, so to sign a document, they would sign with an X. It was called "making their mark."

I invite you to make yours.

I'm an #everydayabolitionist because

_____

_____

_____

Name _____

Date _____

Signature / Mark _____

Or visit everydayabolitionist.co/makeyourmark

Tell somebody

Share your declaration and/or what you're going to do next with someone, with us (everydayabolitionist.co/makeyourmark), with the world, on social media. Get shareable images at everydayabolitionist.co/share

Ante Up

Start a monthly donation to the anti-trafficking charity of your choice.

Continue Learning

- Podcast: Listen to the Ending Human Trafficking podcast by Dr. Sandra Morgan
- Short Book: Read *Start Something to End Trafficking* by David Trotter

Connect with Others Who Care

- Freedom United (freedomunited.org)
- Global Modern Slavery Directory (globalmodernslavery.org)
- Freedom Collaborative (freedomcollaborative.org)
- Everyday Abolitionist Society (everydayabolitionist.co/society)

Join in

- the next Freedom Fortnight (freedomfortnight.org)
- the next Freecember (freecember.org)

Become a Freedom Raiser!

- Freecember (freecember.org)
- Aruna Runs (arunaproject.com)
- Songs Against Slavery (songsagainstslavery.org)
- Dressember (dressember.org)
- Ping Pong-a-thon (pingpongathon.com)

Commit

To ask 1 question, have 1 conversation, to 1 next step you're gonna take.

Fill in the blanks, write it on some paper, share it with someone:

- I'm going to find out _____ (your 1 question).
- I'm going to talk with _____ (your 1 person).
- I'm going to _____ (your 1 next step).

Freedom Forward!

NO ABOLITIONIST IS AN ISLAND

I couldn't have created *Everyday Abolitionist* without the help of multiple communities and the kindness of many strong and loose connections throughout my own relational circles.

A HUGE thanks to:

My wife and kids, who have encouraged and challenged and supported me on this sometimes difficult and often inconvenient and uncertain journey. You're my why.

My friends and family, and everyone who has joined in Freecember and Freedom Fortnight, who have encouraged me and supported me in practical (and impractical!) ways.

Specifically, Brian Berry, whose words I hold on to, thanks for bestfriending me.

Christa Foster Crawford, whose enthusiasm helped me believe I had written something worth sharing.

My editors, cover designer, formatter and everyone who gave supportive critique and feedback, for helping me make this as excellent and professional as possible.

The experts and leaders who gave their endorsements, I am so honored.

The community leaders who shared this resource with your communities, I hope it serves them well.

Sarah Koetsier, whose art expressed and inspired my heart.

Corbett Barr, Chase Reeves, Steph Crowder and all the Fizzlers at Fizzle.co, your insights and support have been invaluable over the past 5 years.

Chandler Bolt, Sean Sumner and the Self-Publishing Mastermind Community at Self-Publishing School, for helping me get from manuscript to *Published.* like a pro.

Donald Miller and StoryBrand for helping me understand how to clarify my message.

Mark Batterson, whose book, *The Circle Maker,* I found on a friend's bookshelf in Zambia while I was writing the manuscript, and every person who prayed for me throughout the writing, revising and publishing process, I'm eternally grateful.

The woman, whose name and organization I can't remember, whose story first broke my heart for the women, children and men exploited in slavery and trafficking, if I could go back to Budapest those years ago, I would wash your feet with my tears.

Everyone who was willing to have conversations with me, listen, teach, empathize and help me on my journey, and all the people who spoke words of encouragement, liked, loved or commented on my social media posts for the book, the cover design, Freecember or Freedom Fortnight, and those who read and critiqued multiple iterations of the manuscript, thanks for helping me have the courage to publish this book and for helping me make it the best I could make it.

Without your support, *Everyday Abolitionist* might not even exist, and it certainly wouldn't be what it is. Thank you for helping me believe this book could be.

Finally, a massive thanks:

To all those who are working to help people live in freedom with dignity and delight, may you have the resources you need to do what you dream of doing.

To the victims & survivors of slavery and trafficking, you're the real heroes. I hope *Everyday Abolitionist* honors you. If at some point it didn't, please forgive me, I'm learning.

To Jesus of Nazareth, who came to set captives free. "Chains shall he break for the slave is our brother"[1]

END NOTES

One

[1] Bales, Kevin, 2012, *Disposable People: New Slavery in the Global Economy*, University of California Press, p. xi

[2] Ewart-James, Joanna, 7th February 2018, personal correspondence, with permission

[3] Keller, Gary with Jay Papasan, 2012, *The One Thing: The Surprisingly Simple Truth Behind Extraordinary Results,* Bard Press, p. 208

Three

[1] Haugen, Gary A. and Victor Boutros, 2014, *The Locust Effect: Why the End of Poverty Requires the End of Violence,* Oxford University Press, p. xv

[2] Headington Institute, "Trauma | Vicarious Trauma," headington-institute.org/topic-areas/125/trauma-and-critical-incidents/246/vicarious-trauma, accessed February 2017

Four

[1] Crawford, Christa Foster, 2015, MD544 Ministry with Sexually Exploited and Trafficked Children, Fuller School of Intercultural Studies, comment in threaded class discussion, with permission

Five

[1] Hope for Justice, "Frequently Asked Questions," hopeforjustice.org/faqs/, accessed March 2017

[2] Grillo, Harmony (Dust), 29th March 2017, personal correspondence, with permission

Seven

[1] Morris, Rob, 2009, North America Asha Forum

Eleven

[1] Gordon, Graham, 2002, *Advocacy Toolkit: Understanding Advocacy*, Tearfund, p. 32

[2] Ibid, p. 31

Chocolate

[1] *Slavery: A Global Investigation*, 2000, True Vision of London

Fourteen

[1] BBC, 2014, *I Bought A Rainforest,* featuring Charlie Hamilton James, charliehamiltonjames.com/i-bought-a-rainforest/

Fifteen

[1] Koetsier, Sarah, *2014, We See The Same Sky*, cast glass and bronze, sarahkoetsier.cargocollective.com/We-See-The-Same-Sky, with permission

Sixteen

[1] Sworn, Helen, November 2017, Asia Region Anti-Trafficking Conference, Bangkok, Thailand, personal conversation, with permission

Eighteen

[1] Bales, Kevin, 2007, *Ending Slavery: How We Free Today's Slaves*. pos. 3395

Nineteen

[1] Anonymous, 5th December 2017, personal email, referenced on freecember.org/stories/best-10-cents-ever, with permission

Epilogue

[1] Freedom United, "About Us: Our Mission," freedomunited.org/about-us/, accessed February 2018

No Abolitionist Is An Island

[1] *O Holy Night*, public domain

THANK YOU!

Thanks SO much for reading *Everyday Abolitionist*!

(All the way to the very end. Wow!)

Questions, Comments, Helpful Suggestions or Just Want to Say Hi?

I'd love to hear from you with any and all the above. It could encourage me or help me make the next version even better.

Visit everydayabolitionist.co/end OR send an email to book@freecember.org

A Request

If you've found *Everyday Abolitionist* helpful, there are two ways you can help someone else out (and help me in the process).

1) Share *Everyday Abolitionist* with a friend.

Is there one person who comes to mind you think might benefit from finding out about this book from you?

Take a moment and share it with them (via email, on social media or over coffee).

You could share:

- a photo or video of you & your copy of the book
- a link to the book
- everydayabolitionist.co/book

If you want to, tag a friend (or a few) you think would be glad to know about this book.

I'd be grateful if you would take a moment to share it with a friend, so they hear about it from someone they know and trust. It could mean someone taking their next steps in freedom.

2) Write an honest review.

By taking a minute or two to give an honest review of *Everyday Abolitionist* on your favorite review platform, you can help people find this resource so they, too, can move from awareness of human trafficking to discovering what they can do to help stop modern slavery.

Thanks for helping people find out about this and for everything you're doing to move freedom forward, everyday abolitionist!

Made in the USA
San Bernardino, CA
23 March 2019